ARTWORK DESIGNED BY JENNIFER ROSS

COVER DESCRIPTION WRITTEN BY NATALIE HAMINGSON

COVER QUOTE CITATION: TUPAC SHAKUR. (N.D.) BRAINYQUOTE.COM. RE-TRIEVED JANUARY 2, 2016 FROM BRAINYQUOTE.COM. (WEB).

ISBN-10: 1522843264

ISBN-13: 9781522843269

SECOND EDITION

D1465985

AN ARTICLE, BY JABARI MILLER

I HAVE HAD THE PLEASURE OF KNOWING ABDUL FATTAH ISMAIL SINCE AN EXCURSION ONCE UPON A TIME IN AFRICA CIRCA 2000. FROM THEN, HE SHARED WORDS WITH ME. WORDS THAT BROUGHT LAUGHTER, THAT MADE ME SHAKE MY HEAD AND ALSO CHALLENGED ME TO REFLECT AND CONSIDER. WORDS HELD TOGETHER IN SIMPLE HONESTY, REVOLUTION AND BROTHERHOOD. ALTHOUGH AN ISMAIL, I TESTIFY TO THE FACT THIS BROTHER HAS ALWAYS BEEN A SMITH. COULD IT HAVE BEEN THE RESULT OF HAVING DEMANDING AFRICAN PARENTS, AN INNATE LOVE OF KNOWLEDGE, A HEART THAT HEARS PEOPLE, OR EYES THAT SEE TRUTH THROUGH A NATIVE LENS? MAYBE IT'S DUE TO THE VIBRATIONS OF THE SUBWAYS OR SUN DRIED DRUMS, OR HUMS OF PLANE ENGINES. IN ESSENCE, EXTENDED SYLLABLES IS A DIRECT REFLECTION OF ABDUL'S SHARP, WITTY, FRESH, CLASSIC, CONSCIOUS, VIVID, AND AUTHENTIC SELF. NO PRESERVATIVES ADDED ...OR NEEDED.

EXTENDED SYLLABLES IS NOTHING LESS THAN A FUSION OF SENTIENT WORLDLY WINDS, JOURNEYING FROM LABORATORIES OF THOUGHT TO INNER CITY CUTS, SNAPS OF NY LANDSCAPES, RESONATING TAPESTRIES OF REAL, SHADES OF YESTERDAY'S ECHOES AND SPICE MARKETS IN EGYPT; ALL CAUGHT AT ECCENTRIC ANGLES. PIECES LIKE DUKE OF YORK, MY OWN MILITARY, FOG AND SUN SITTING IN A TREE, MALCOLM WOULD BE PROUD, AND FLASH.EYEBROWS.SPAN (TO NAME A FEW OF MY FAVORITES) IN THE WORDS OF ABDUL, "(IT) WILL EDUCATE, IT WILL INSPIRE".

WHAT IS IT WHEN WORDS STRETCH FORTH TO SATISFY A HUNGER YOU HAD NOT QUITE REALIZED WAS BREWING IN THE MIND? WHEN THOSE WORDS ARE FROM A BROTHER, OR SISTER, HOW MUCH GREATER IS THE BLESSING?

IN CLOSING, I WISH TO THANK ABDUL FOR HIS COURAGE AND DETERMINA-
TION IN HARNESSING HIS GIFT IN BEING THE "BEST GIFTER". IT IS ALSO AN
HONOR TO GREET YOU AT THE GATES AND INTRODUCE TO YOU THESE
LANGSTON-LIKE EXTENDED SYLLABLES. THERE IS ALWAYS A WITNESS
FROM THE SECOND A STONE IS CAST. ENJOY.

<u>AMPERSANDS (&)</u>

TO ALL MY SOLDIERS OF LOVE AND WISDOM. MAYBE YOU TOO.

EXTENDED SYLLABLES

LEW ALCINDOR

KAREEM ABDUL-JABBAR

YOU GLIDE ON IN A CAR

STRIDE TO THE LEFT

DUCK RIGHT, SKY HOOK

YOU'RE KAREEM ABDUL-JABBAR

KAREEM ABDUL-JABBAR

YOU BUY COORS AT THE BAR

DIP, SHAKE RIGHT

HEAD FAKE

JUMP SHOT

YOU'RE KAREEM ABDUL-JABBAR

KAREEM ABDUL-JABBAR

YOUR CONVERSE HAS ONE STAR

88 WINS, 6 RINGS, 3 PLAQUES

YOU'RE KAREEM ABDUL-JABBAR

BUFFALO SOLDIER, BALD HEAD RASTA, KAREEM ABDUL-JABBAR

OPINION WRITER, SURE SHOT CALLER, KAREEM ABDUL-JABBAR

HARLEM, NEW YORK. LA FOR LIFE.

I WILL NOT APOLOGIZE

THE APOLOGY

ACCEPTED

THE APOLOGY

FORTHCOMING

THE APOLOGY

HOLD ON

THE APOLOGY

SAY WHAT?

THE APOLOGY

SURE

THE APOLOGY

FOR WHY?

THE APOLOGY

NOT A THANG

THE APOLOGY

REALLY?

THE APOLOGY

WORD

THE APOLOGY

EXPECTED

THE APOLOGY

OKAY

THE APOLOGY

MAYBE

THE APOLOGY

BECAUSE OF THAT

THE APOLOGY

NOT QUITE

SORRY I WILL NOT APOLOGIZE

OLD TEA PARTY BAGS

TO THE LAST STRIKE

DOWN AND OUT

THE TEA PARTY DIGS IN THE TWITTER BOWL

LAST CHARACTER AND ALL

A SKULL FILLED WITH FALSE ENTITLEMENT

BIRTHED FROM THE DAYS OF MICHELANGELO

WHO PAINTED THEIR ALLEGED SUPERIORITY?

WHEN THE FUMES DRIPPED INTO THE BLOOD OF CONSTANTINE

WHERE IDEAS OF WESTERN CIVILIZATION WERE BIRTHED

HOW SLAVES OF YORE WERE BRUSHED OFF

WITH A SWORD THEN

THEY THRUST A PICKET SIGN TODAY

THREATENED BY PURE CIVIC DUTY

ONCE A PILLAR OF SOCIOLOGICAL INNOVATION

DARING TODAY TO PROJECT CITY REGENERATION

INSTEAD OF OFFBEAT REPARATIONS

LIKE A VAPID ALASKAN VIXEN

TO MAXIMIZE REALITY

SO THAT DEMOGRAPHIC ECONOMY

CAN SLOW STOCK ATROPHY

TOPICAL COVERAGE OF LATENT THREATS

TO THE NATURE

OF BLATANT REPUBLICANISM

THAT RUNS FROM THE AGE OF AQUARIUS

IN A CLOUD OF SELF-FLAGELLATION

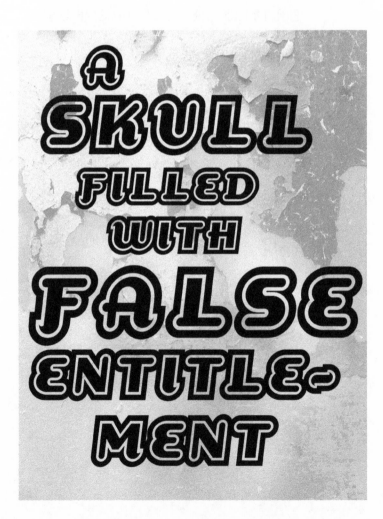

SLASHONESQUE

STEVE BIKO BROKE THE RULES

BECAUSE THE RULES OF APARTHEID NEEDED TO BE BROKEN

SOMETIMES, BREAKING THE RULES IS BAD

OFTENTIMES, SOME GET ALL THE BREAKS

A BROKE SLAVE HAS BUSTED POCKETS

THAT INDOMITABLE SPIRIT, THOUGH, BROKE THE CHAINS

AS BROKEN IRON FELL TO THE SOIL

DIGITAL WIRES TODAY ARE BREAKING BOUNDARIES

OF THE NATION-STATE, WHO BREAKS TO SAVE DYING CURRENCY?

AFTER ISSUING BROKE LOAN DOCUMENTS

LEAVING HOMES BROKEN IN SPIRIT WORLDWIDE

BREAKING BAD DOES PAY FOR TELEVISION ADS

BRYAN CRANSTON BREAKS OUT OF MALCOM'S MIDDLE ON TOP

BEING BROKE IS EATING CEREAL WITH A FORK TO SAVE MILK

IN A BROKEN MOONLIGHT

WHERE THE FIRE IS BREAKING IN A DANCE

AN EVEN SPLIT FROM THE LAND

MARS, THEN JUPITER

YOU SHAVE THE FACE OF YESTERDAY

YOUR CITY EYELIDS STOP AND START

YOUR OLD BOSS LIVES INSIDE YOUR HEAD

YOUR SHOWERHEAD STREAMS LIVE SLOW CHILLS

MONTHS OF RED

YOU STILL WANT A FLAME FROM HIGH SCHOOL

YOUR SUBWAY SEAT HOLDS BIG RAINDROPS

YOUR PRICE TAG READS $2.99

YOUR SOCKS HAVE TOE HOLES IN BOTH OF THEM

MONTHS OF RED

YOUR COLLEAGUES DON'T TRUST YOU ONCE

YOUR WORK OUTFIT IS JUST SOME CLOTHES

YOUR SWEAT GLANDS DON'T WORK INDOORS

YOUR HEART BEATS SLOWER THAN DUB SACKS

MONTHS OF RED

YOU ARE THE KING OF DILETTANTES

YOU EAT THE BREAD OF STALE AND DRY

YOU PLAY A SILENT WOOD OBOE

YOU SINK DEEPER THAN YOU KNOW

MONTHS OF RED

MIDNIGHT SPHERE

KNOWING THE ENEMY

TAKES THE OPEN SIXTH SENSE

SIMMERING, SUGARY

TAKING IT BRIEFLY

KILLING YOUR SPRING DREAMS

I STILL LAUGH OUT LOUD

AS ONE

TEASING YOUR MEMORIES

DYING TO FLY THROUGH BREEZE

I DRIVE ON THE TARMAC

WITH NERVES THAT HOLD STILL

SHAKING STAR POETRY

BOUNCE WITH CACOPHONY

I TAKE, YOUR CLOUDS

AND BLOW THEM TO BITS

PAST THE VEINS, PHYSICALLY

DARKENED WITH ANCESTRY

BUSINESS, ONLY, STRICTLY

NIGHTS IN WHITE NOTEBOOKS

I DRAW THE ACRONYM

VERB, ADVERB

ADJECTIVE, NOUN, PLACE

PREDICATE

TO A PAGE OF SUBSTANCE

A STYLE WARS MAGNET

TWIRLED INTO A PREFIX

PAIR YOUR DOUBLE HELIX

MIC TEST, MIC TEST

MIX MASTER MIKE

LICK TO TASTE

TEST MINDS THRICE TIME

TURN UP, TWO HANDS

SWING LEFT, DUCK RIGHT

CATCH THE CAB

FARE DUE, ONE WAY

FOR THE 22

SECOND SENTRY

SECOND ON THE AVE

BEFORE NIGHT FALLS

NIGHTMARES

THE SONG REMAINS THE SAME

THE VIDEOS PAUSE, THEN PLAY

THE COLORS

MUDDY OVER HERE

SHARP PIXELS AT THAT

THE FOYER BEEPS WITH BOOST MOBILE

FINGERNAILS TAP ON THE WINDOW

TO SCRATCH AND CLAW YOUR DREAMS

INTO SUBMISSION

WHILE YOU DROP YOUR STUB OF ADMISSION

INTO THE TRASH CAN

THAT SITS ON THE CORNER

SCRATCHED AND SNIFFED

REGRETS COME TO TRIAL IN WONDERLAND

THE MIRRORS IN YOUR DREAM

REFLECT THE GHOSTS OF YOU

THAT LINGERS ON THE TIP OF YOUR TONGUE

SHAKING, AS YOUR WORLD STIRS

DRILLBITS

IN THOSE MINES

THE AIR AIN'T NEW

TUNA CANS ARE FAR AND FEW

AY DIO

NO HOPE

DIGGING FOR THE COPPER BLUE

SAN JOSE BLOCKS THE SKY VIEW

FUTURES

UNKNOWN

CHINA GROWS FROM DAY TO DAY

CHILE CLAWS FOR LITTLE PAY

HOW SO?

NO HAGO

FACES LIKE THE MAGNUM, TRUE

URZUA, HE LEADS, HE DO

POTS OF GOLD

A TODOS

PONY EXPRESS

PORT TO PORT

ROAD TO ROAD

T THROUGH BOSTON

YOU SEE THAT

YOU ARE INVITED

TO ANYONE

YOU ARE INVITED

TO THANK THE LOVED

YOU ARE INVITED

TO BREAK THE RULES

YOU ARE INVITED

TO LOATHE THE DAY

YOU ARE INVITED

TO FALL DOWN TWICE

YOU ARE INVITED

TO DEBATE AND CURSE

YOU ARE INVITED

TO CHAT AND CHEW

YOU ARE INVITED

TO HOLD ME TIGHT

YOU ARE INVITED

FOR ALL TIMES

YOU ARE INVITED

TO PLANT THOSE FRUITS

YOU ARE INVITED

TO SEEK KNOWLEDGE

YOU ARE INVITED

TO LAUGH ALL DAY

YOU ARE INVITED

TO STOP TALKING

YOU ARE INVITED

TO STOP CRYING

YOU ARE INVITED

TO KISS AND TELL

YOU ARE INVITED

TO CLIMB, THEN STAND

YOU ARE INVITED

FOR ALL TIMES

YOU ARE INVITED

TO MAKE THE MOLD

YOU ARE INVITED

TO HIDE FOREVER

YOU ARE INVITED

TO BE A FAT ASS

YOU ARE INVITED

TO LEAP, THEN FLY

YOU ARE INVITED

TO ANYONE

YOU ARE INVITED

FOR ALL TIMES

KILLA COLON

IN FIRST GRADE

WE SALUTED YOUR JOURNEYS

WE CELEBRATED WITH COSTUMES

WE OBSERVED THE DAY BY CLOSING

THEN LATER ON IN GRADE SCHOOL

WE OPENED UP

AND STAYED THAT WAY

A FRIEND TOLD ME ABOUT THE WAY

YOU DOGGED YOUR KIND AND MINE

THE PEOPLE'S HISTORY SPOKE TO THE IGNANT

CONFIRMING WHAT WE SUSPECTED

DESPITE WHAT WE KNOW NOW

THE CITY SLOWS DOWN

TO IGNORE THE FIGHT AGAINST THE MIND

LETTING THE LIE WIN

EVEN THOUGH HISTORY AND ARTIFACTS

REMAIN TRUE

PARTNERED WITH LORE

CARD STOCK

WE ONCE WALKED IN SCRANTON FOR A FEW DAYS

SITTING IN A CONFERENCE ROOM AT TIMES BETWEEN

WE EVEN WALKED BETWEEN THE CAMPUS COURTYARDS

DUSTED WITH COAL MOUNTAIN WISPS

BEFORE LEBRON, WE WERE WITNESSES IN CLEVELAND

AT THE SAME TIME, BUT NOT IN THE SAME ROOM

WE EASILY CHATTED ONLINE

I TYPED A THOUSAND HEARTBEATS PER KEYSTROKE

A STREETCAR NAMED AND FILLED WITH DESIRE

YOU MOVED TO THE EMERALD ISLE

FROM THE ANDEAN CHILEAN ARCHIPELAGO

I BUILD A PLAN TO TAKE GOTHAM

YOU DIRECTLY CARE FOR THE CORE

WITH JEAN VANIER

TODAY, I WRITE TO YOU IN TEN WORDS PER HAND GLIDE

A TRILLION SENSES IN ONE DIRECTION

ON CARD STOCK

BALLPOINT: BLACK INK

FINELY STROKED

A SCREW SPROUTING FROM THE LAWN

YOU COULD STUDY

RECONSTRUCTION

SEGREGATION

MISCEGENATION

FED LEGISLATION

OLD PATIENCE

DRAWS STILL ANIMATION

AND NOT SPARK ANOTHER OWL

RESTING ON AN IPAD

SAD FROM THE LOST HOURS

OF VIRAL DEPRAVEMENT

TALKING AT STARBUCKS

IN LAYMAN'S TERMS

THOSE LAID FREE CONNECTIONS

SCATTERED IN GREY PEWS

THE BLACK SQUIRREL OF BEDOUIN

DUST TICKLED YOUR CORNEA

WHICH FOUGHT MORE THAN FREE PARTICLES

THEY BATTED THEMSELVES

FROM IMAGES MADE INTO MEMORY

ONCE, AN EMBARRASSMENT OF ACTION

ACTS OF DETERMINATION

LUNGES OF PAIN

AT YOUR FURRY BRETHREN

THEM OF AN AUBURN HUE

GUFFAWING THAT YOU WERE DARKER THAN BLUE

YOU HAD BEEN DISPLACED LIKE THE NAVAJO

AN ODD RELIC IN SPACES OF BROOKLYN

OVER THE ANTICS ON ATLANTIC

SPINNING YOUR REVENGE THEATRICS, AS YOU LIKE IT

THE LOVE OF WIRE CRAWLING

TAPPED, THOSE FEARS OF HEIGHTS

FLOWING, THE RIVER OF REVENGE

HUSTLE, THOSE RODENT BRETHREN

DARING TO GRIN IN THE TENT

SENSE WITH COINS

ATTACK OF THE CURRENCIES

SIBLINGS YEN AND YUAN

TACK ON MORE WESTERN ANGST

UNLIKE A TICKY TACK FOUL

FROM ERICK DAMPIER

ONE SENATOR WANTS TO TAX

THOSE SIBLINGS

WHO DARE TO TACK OUR LIVING ROOMS AND SHOULDERS

FULL OF CLOTH, BLOCKS OF DIGITAL

THEN TACKLE OUR STOMACHS

WITH KOBE BEEF AND TACTILE VEGGIES

A TACK ON OUR BALANCE SHEETS

PRESSED WITH A THUMB

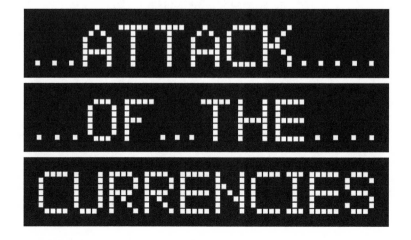

THE FLOOD

I STAYED UP LATE

READING UNTIL OLD

IT ROSE ABOVE THE WHITE SANDS OF MALIBU

THE SUPER CLEANED UP THE FOYER

THE PUGET SOUND FLOATED NOTES ABOVE THE WASHINGTON FIRS

I PICKED UP MY NEWSPAPERS FROM THE STOOP

THE MISSISSIPPI RIVER LEAKED ACROSS THE HEARTLAND

KETTLES BOIL, THEN POUR INTO CUPS AND BOWLS

THE GULF OF MEXICO BOILED OUT THE DEEP SOUTH

I GREET MY ROOMMATE

THE RIO GRANDE VIENE MAS GRANDE

I SPIN A WEB WITH FLOSS

A TOOTHBRUSH GLIDES ACROSS MY MOLARS

THE BRONX RESERVOIR MEETS UP AT A PARTY

WITH THE EAST AND AND HUDSON RIVERS

HOSTED BY THE ATLANTIC

THE WAVES CAME FROM ALL CORNERS

FOR THIS MOMENT

THEY MOVE DOWNTOWN

I OPEN MY DOOR

THEY ARREST MY BODY

I KICK AND PUSH

I PULL UP

THEY PULL DOWN

I PULL UP HARDER

THEY PUSH AND PULL DOWN

I FLATTEN ON A FORD F-150 BED

OXYGEN RESTORED

ESCAPE COMPLETE

OXYGEN RESTORED ESCAPE COMPLETE

ESCARGOT

MOVING

THROUGH THE STETHOSCOPE OF FEAR

PUNISH WALLS WITH GRIPPED FIST

DRY STENCH OF WHEAT BEER

RAGING

PART MAN, FULL AMAZEMENT

MINTY FRESH LEAVES

PUNCH TYSON IN THE BASEMENT

TRADING

DECAY OF NEW MILLENNIUMS

COMMODITY OF COPPER

CONDUCT HEAT CANNED

BY THE ALUMINUM

DRIVING

PUSH STONES TO THE SIDE

POLISHED TOENAIL SCENT

UNGLUED, SHOT WITH BROMIDE

A SNAIL'S PACE

DUKE OF YORK

THE CITY IS HERE

PLAYS THE SCENE OF WONDERTOWN

AS ALWAYS

I JUST WALK AROUND IT

FROM STRIDE TO STRIDE

WHILE ITS DEATH HAS BEEN PROCLAIMED SINCE ITS BEGINNING

BEFORE THE IROQUOIS

DUTCH ARCHITECTS

ENGLISH TRADERS

DON DRAPER

BRET EASTON ELLIS

RALPH ELLISON

DR. JONATHAN GOLOB

YOUR FAVORITE DEEJAYS

SOME CATHOLIC PRIESTS

YOUR EX PARTNERS

PHILLY FOLKS

CALI HEADS

MIDWEST BOYS

MIAMI MUJERES

BUT THE END NEVER SEEMS IN SIGHT

MR. SOFTEE WHISTLES

DUKE ELLINGTON STILL TAKES THE A TRAIN AS A FRIENDLY GHOST

CENTRAL PARK GLISTENS IN THE WINTER ICE

I STILL LIVE IN THE SAME BUILDING, SAME CRIB

SAME NUMBERS

WOMEN STILL LINE UP AT 4 PM FOR THE BARNEY'S WAREHOUSE SALE

THEN SLINK INTO SWEATY CABS AT SPRING STREET

SOME BUY PARLIAMENTS FIRST

ONE OF THEM STEALS BIT-O-HONEY

TO PUT OUT HER HUNGER

HEARD THROUGH HER EYELASH

SENSED BY THE UNSMITTEN

WE LOVE YOU FOR MANY REASONS

THEY LEAVE YOU FOR ONE REASON

THEY CAN'T HANG

MY COCOA CURE

I ONCE KNEW A MAN

WHO WOULD WALK THE LINE

PLUCK A COCOA BEAN

WITH A GHANA SMILE

HE WOULD GIVE THE BEAN

GRIPPED NOT BUT TWICE

HER LIPS TOUCH THE BEAN

MELTING IT AT ONCE

ONE DAY, AN EXPLORER

FROM WHENCE UNCLEAR

SHOOK THE TREES SIDEWAYS

FROM THERE OUT TO HERE

CHILDREN IN BERLIN

SMILE AT NEWLYWED BARS

COLORED COSTUMES TAPED

NAMED LINDT AND MARS

THE FIRE THIS TIME

SINGED AZTEC TONGUES

WHICH WHISPERED, THRICE SNICKERED

AT MOVING GUMS

THE FOOTSIE RAISES IT

FROM QUID UP TO P

LOVE AND COCOA

SHINES FROM SEA TO SEA

RAISINS

LEGEND SAYS THAT CURIOSITY

KILLED THE CAT

OF COURSE CURIOSITY KILLED IT

BECAUSE THE CAT CANNOT

TRANSCEND ITS SENSES

IT LIVES BY SIGHT

IT DIES BY SIGHT

LOOKS CAN KILL

FOR A CAT

THE MIND OF HUMANS

FEELS CURIOSITY

IT STRIPS NEUROSES DRY

TO REST IN THE PARIETAL LOBE

AMONG THE FLASHES OF YELLOW

ABOUT THOSE GOLDEN HUMS

ACCESSED FROM YOUR RADIO DIAL

ADDED TO YOUR SMELL OF VIOLETS

AFTER THE SUN MADE IT GLOW ORANGE

A PARTING OF YOUR EYELIDS LEAVE BLURRED, DANCING PUPILS ALONE

ASKING QUESTIONS

ROLLING THE DICE

FOR A BIG CRAYOLA BOX

A CONDUIT FOR ITS COUSIN

ELECTRICITY

TO LIGHT YOUR EARLOBE

SINCE NO ONE REALLY DIES

EVER

THE MICROSOFT TOUCH

TWICE UPON TWO TIMES

REALLY LONG AGO

AN ALLEN AND GATES

BUILD VOLTRON

FROM HEAD TO TOE

MICROSERFS RADIATE ELECTROWAVES

CHANGE PIXELS THREE DEGREES

MR. GATES WAS OUT TO PLEASE

WITH GEEK SMARTS

NO COLLEGE DEGREE

WE ALL AGREED THAT THE REVOLUTION OF LABOR WOULD MINIMIZE

BETWEEN BIG AND SMALL IN MORE DIMENSIONS

UNDETERRED BY HUMAN ERROR

EAT THE FRIED EYES

ONCE SUNNY, NOW SIDE UP

TODAY, THE REVOLUTION NEED NOT BE TELEVISED

THE SEQUEL HAS PASSED US EVERY MILLISECOND

WITHOUT A SIGHT

WITH PLENTY OF SOUND

BLUE COUNTRY HILLS

I'VE BEEN AROUND AND AROUND

AND I'VE GOT SOMEWHERE TO GO NOW

BUT THE FUNNY THING IS THAT

WHEN I'M GONE

I'LL WONDER

I'LL SNOOZE

I'LL GET SOIL IN MY FINGERNAILS

THE GRASS WILL POKE MY HIPS AND PINKIE TOES

THE DARKNESS OF MY EYELIDS STAYS GRAY

THE SUN GLOWS BURNT SIENNA

WHEN I OPEN UP THE LENSES

BUT I PAID MY DEBT

ON TIME

I INVESTED MY HANDS

SO IT'S OVER NOW

YOU NEVER BEEN ABLE

TO CASH RIGHT OUT

BALANCE THE TILL

BECAUSE IT'S OVER NOW

I PAY MY DEBTS

ON TIME

I PAID MY DEBT

IN TIME

400 METER DASH

I WISH THAT I HAD INDEPENDENCE

WANT TO FREELANCE

THEN DANCE TO THE MUSIC

NOT A CHANCE

OF HAPPENSTANCE

IN OUR WORLD AMBIVALENCE

SPIT SOME LONG PARLANCE

CIRCLE OUT ONE ARMSTRONG

ADVANCE IN THE MOONLIGHT

GUIDE BY PROGRESS

WORD TO DELIVERANCE

BREAKING WOOD BLOCKS

JUMPING FENCES

INTO THE WHITE

STRIPS OF COHESION

SLIDE IN URBAN BASES

A SLICK DHARMA BUM

TEN KMS ON OVER

3000 MILES OUT

EXISTENTIAL TREADMILLS

BURNING THE LUMBERJACK LOGS

EXISTENTIAL TREADMILLS

RUNNING ON A FULL TANK

DICKENS' EXPECTATIONS

MET ONCE THERE BEFORE

BREAK ON OUT OF THE HUDDLE

THROWING DEEP TO SCORE

EXISTENTIAL TREADMILLS

A SNEAK ATTACK CHILLS YOUR SPINE

EXISTENTIAL TREADMILLS

RUNNING ON A FULL TANK

DRUM FLICKERS AND FLICKS

YELLOW LINES RUN

FROM EAST TO WEST

LONGITUDE

LATITUDE

TO SOOTHE YOUR IRIS

LIKE BAMBOO LEAVES

LIKE NIGHTS IN LONDON

LIKE HITS OF SUNSHINE

LIKE FLUTES FROM FREETOWN

WITH ROOTS IN BEET FIELDS

BUT.....

WE NEVER RIDE

OLLY OLLY

OXEN FREE

WE TAKE ALL THE BREAD

SHOVE IT DOWN

BURP PLEASANTRIES

TOO LITTLE

TOO LATE

TO RIDE

OLLY OLLY

OXEN FREE

SILLY ME

GREAT EXPECTATIONS

I REMEMBER WE MET UP ONE NIGHT IN THE BEND

IN DEBAUCHERY

OUT BY THE BASKETBALL RIM

OFF THE RAINY DECK

THE PARTY STARTED

IT LASTED FOR 17 YEARS

I TRIED TO LET YOU GO

IN SO MANY WAYS

I DUMPED YOU IN DEUTSCHLAND

I TOSSED THE IMAGES

DIGITAL AND UNCONSCIOUS

ONLY TO HAVE THEM SEEP BACK INTO MY SKULL

ONLY TO HAVE YOU COME BACK LIKE JASON TO CRYSTAL LAKE

SIPHONING MY WILLPOWER

THROUGH GLASSES AND PINTS

A FEAST ON THE SCIATICA

A MELLOW AFTER THE FEAST

BUT I REALIZED THAT YOU WERE REALLY

JUST A FIGMENT OF MY SILLY IMAGINATION

KIND OF LIKE MANY ROMANCES

THAT WERE CREATED AND DISSIPATED

NOT UNLIKE MATTER

I DON'T NEED YOU

I NEVER REALLY WANTED YOU

I WAS JUST EASILY TEMPTED

THESE DAYS, MORE TRICKS ARE NECESSARY

LET'S SEE WHAT YOU HAVE

I'M READY TO BATTLE

<u>FOG AND SUN SITTING IN A TREE</u>

AN ACTIVIST

A VERBALIST

TRADE ANALYST

PEACE TERRORIST

TECH SCIENTIST

CITY SOCIOLOGIST

URBAN PSYCHOLOGIST

CUNNYLINGUIST

EPICURIST

FLAMBOASTIST

HORTICULTURALIST

SPORTS PHYSICIST

EXHIBITIONIST

MACROENVIRONMENTALIST

MYSTERIOUS COUNTENANCE

FUTURIST

THE YAY

FATHER MC

A TISKET

A TASKET

A GULF COAST GASKET

BLOWN TO SMITHEREENS

DROPS CAREEN OFF PRIMED WALLS

NEWLY INSTALLED WITH DRY FAITH

FAITH THAT DRIED THE PEOPLE'S TEARS

FAITH THAT CALMED THE WOUNDS

FROM THE GALES WHIPPING THE MISSISSIPPI JELLYFISH

AUNT KATRINA'S MEAN OLD DEATH WISH

ONE NIGHT, BP FISHES FOR TROUBLE

INVITES VANESSA OVER, A JEOPARDY DOUBLE

AFTER THE SAINTS MARCHED IN, RIDING COLTS

FILLING THE HOUSE WITH HURRICANES FROM YOURS TRULY, PAT O'BRIEN

HAND GRENADES IN GREEN JUICE

LOBBED WITH TABASCO HEAT

A BOURBON STREET SWAP MEET

CUPID THROWS DRUNKEN STARS

NESSA OPENS UP TOO FAR

START TO KISS MEN

STAINING UP SALT BEARDS

BEFORE THEY HIT BARS

THEY WERE IT

HER PALMS OF OIL SAID SO

MEN RUN TO KISS VANESSA BACK

SHE'S IT

THEN SHE RUNS TO KISS OBAMA

HE SAYS, "NOPE, I DON'T DRIVE ANYMORE."

VANESSA STILL HAS IT

SWAMP FOLK GOT IT AGAIN

MIKHAIL PHRUSCHEV

I SNUCK INTO THE TENT AT BRYANT PARK

I USED TO LOVE COCA-COLA

I HAD A LONG, INCREDIBLE RELATIONSHIP WITH DARRYL STRAWBERRY

I STILL HANG OUT WITH DOC EVERY NOW AND THEN

I CRASHED THIS WICKED GRADUATION PARTY ON PARK AVENUE THIS SUNDAY

I DRESS UP AS A POWDERED DONUT FROM TIME TO TIME

I TRAVEL ALL OVER THE WORLD

I SWIM IN THE SEVEN SEAS

I AM ALWAYS LOOKING FOR SOMEONE

I ALWAYS NEED SOMETHING

I ONCE FUCKED YOUR GIRLFRIEND

I NEVER TOLD YOU ABOUT THAT WEEKEND

BECAUSE I ALWAYS WANTED YOUR APPROVAL

FILLED WITH WORDS BECOMING LINES

LINES GROOMED INTO THOUGHTS

THOUGHTS SPROUTING INTO DREAMS

OF HEAVEN, BY DAY, AND BY NIGHT

BUT IT'S NOT YOU

IT'S NOT ME EITHER

IT'S THE MYSTERY FORCE

CREATED BY THE BIG BANG THEORY

A LOVER OF OMNIVORES

SUCCULENT CARNIVORES

PASSIONATELY DISSIN HERBIVORES

WHO INTRODUCED ME TO YOU

HOW DARE HE

NEUROSURGERY

I DON'T CARE WHAT HE DOES

I DON'T CARE WHAT SHE SAYS

WRITERS AND PHOTOGRAPHERS

IT'S NOT FOR ME TO KNOW

IT'S NOT FOR ME TO KNOW

MY ALARM CLOCK, NATURALIZED

CURRENCY EBBS AND FLOWS

GERMANY SHORT SELLS HOPE

SO SHIFTING, THAT CIRCLE

SO SHIFTING, THAT CIRCLE

THE POLITICS OF THE STREET

POLYMORPH FROM STRIDE TO EYE

SENATE BUILDS A BRICK LABYRINTH

I WISH I COULD CARE

I WISH I COULD CARE

THE TOUR BUS KICKS UP DIRT

CRUSHING CHALK AT 75

GUITARS SCREAM WITH NO PLUCKS

MY VOCALS ARE BLOCKED

MY VOCALS ARE BLOCKED

I CAN HUM OUT TUNES WITH YOU

BUT WHAT'S THE USE

YOUR EARS ARE QUIET

MY FLUTE DANCES LIKE THAT BIRD

THE WOODMAN

WOODY THE PECKER

SENSED, HEARD, BELIEVED

YEAH

BETWEEN THE STOPS

A FIRST ROUND KNOCKOUT

FIRST TIME KNOCKING

THAT ONE FLOPPED

OUT THE BOX

CREMATION

IT'S HARD TO BE FREE

TRUTH BE TOLD, THE STATION

DOORS CLOSING NOW, ONE-TWO-THREE

DEFLATION

I WRITE A MILE A MINUTE

SPEEDING HIGH, TABLATION

3-2-1-CONTACT

OVER HEADS

INVASION

CRISP VEGETABLES

IF YOU THOUGHT ABOUT IT

THEN PANTOMIMED IT

BEFORE DREAMING OF METHOD

YOU COULD HAVE ACTED IT OUT

AT MORNINGSIDE PARK

TO WARM UP FOR SHAKESPEARE

IF YOU WANTED TO GET THERE

USING TWO ARMS AND THREE EYES

SWIVELED ON TWO HIPS AND LEGS

YOU COULD HAVE BEEN THE BICYCLE THIEF

IF YOU TALKED ABOUT IT

IN REAL IBSEN STEREO SOUND

BRACED WITH MONO FROM THE BEATLES

NOTED BY THE ISLEY BROTHERS

CO-SIGNED BY GEORGE DUKE

WITH A CYLINDRICAL PEN

IN A FLOOP DE LOOP SCRIPT

FLIPPED, WHEN CLAY GETS HIS REVENGE

ON LULA IN THE DUTCHMAN

WRITTEN BY AMIRI BARAKA

CAN YOU FEEL THAT?

YOU CAN DO IT

SCROOGE MCDUCK HITS CENTURY 21

ANALYZE THIS STATISTIC

CROSSING THE SECTION

TIME AFTER TIME IN A SERIES

TRUE WORLD POLICY

UNDER MY THUMB

LIKE A TESTIFY FROM TEAM GOLDMAN

ROLLING LIKE A STONE

A FICTIONAL SET OF EARNINGS

UNRETAINED BY CAPITAL MARKETS

UNABLE TO SPEND THEM WITH THE SPEED OF SOUND

BUT THE SCIENCE OF LIGHT

THAT HEAT TURNED REAL

A PAGE TURNED TO BLUE

SAD HAIRED POLITICIANS TALKED REAL

THE WALL STREET JOURNAL PRINTED EXTRA

NOT ORDINARY

A NICKEL FOR YOUR DIME

ONE EXAM IS DONE

MY FAVORITE TEAMS LOST TODAY

THIRST IS SO CRAZY

NEW AND OLD AMSTERDAM

BELOW THE GEORGE WASHINGTON BRIDGE

BENEATH THE CRISP BLUE PLACE MAT OF SKY

BODEGAS WEATHER THE SNOW, RAIN, AND SLEET

PASSING OUT HAMS WITH CHEESE

SNEAKING LOOSE CIGARETTES INTO WORN HANDS

NEIGHBORHOOD BARS SHAKE TO MERENGUE

TUBE TOPS AND ANKLE BRACELETS STRETCHED TO THERE

HAIR AND NAIL REPAIR

ALWAYS INCLUDED

TO GRAB STREET POLYESTER AND SYNTHETICS

THE PART OF MANGO

THAT STIRS THE STRAWBERRY

FOR THE CUP DOST DRINKETH

THOUST GREEN LEAVES BURNETH

THE CORNERS OF 157 TO 197

CREME OF THE CREAM

SOMEDAY, SOMEHOW

CHEEKS STRONG WITH STRONG BEAMS

LIGHT

DARK

LIGHT

FAT JACARANDAS

SOMEDAY, SOMEHOW

THIS BOOK WILL BE AN OLD DREAM

BLACK

WHITE

FADE

BRIGHT IPAD CANVAS

SOMEDAY, SOMEHOW

FISTS FLY IN A CROSS STREAM

LEFT

RIGHT

LEFT

FULL OF SOUND AND FURY

SOMEDAY, SOMEHOW

YOU'LL WHISPER SOMETHING TO ME

TART

TENSE

FOUL

SOME SUSPECT SUSPENSE

SOMEDAY, SOMEHOW

WITH THE MASERATI

CRUISE

THROUGH

DRY

DANK ENDLESS BADLANDS

THESE DAYS ARE SPRY

THE AEGEAN SEA OF RED

I COULD SAY THAT I'M SURPRISED

FRANCE AND GERMANY SAID NO WAY

THEN AFTER FURTHER REVIEW, THE WORDS DID NOT STAND

ANALYSTS BATTLE THE BAND

MINE, THEY DO NOT

NEITHER DO THE POLITICS OF SLAVE ECONOMY

TINGED WITH GREEK PHYSIOLOGY

THE IMF, HMPH, NO ACCOUNTABILITY

THEY DO NOT RELIEVE THE WORLD BURDENS

FROM SECOND TO THIRD BASE

SLIDING IN WITH CHEMICAL STIMULATIONS

DUSTING VILLAGES BUILT TOUGH LIKE FORD

LOWERING EXPECTATIONS OF LIVES TAUGHT MINIMALLY

WRITING NEW TALES OF GREEK MYTHOLOGY

GRAND BAILOUT, MINOR DISASTER

SO THEY SAY

THEN LAY ON THEIR BEACHES, SUCKING OLIVES

TICKLING GODDESSES

OILED WITH DECADENCE AND SALT

AN ILLUSION OF LORE AND LUST

SUNG BY THE SEA OF CRETE

DEAR DOROTHY

I HAD NEVER MET YOU

THEREFORE, I HAVEN'T SEEN YOU

BUT WE GOT ACQUAINTED

THROUGH FOLK TALES

TOLD IN CLASS

IN FEBRUARY

OF YOUR WISDOM

OF YOUR COURAGE

ON THE ROADS

TOBACCO AND DAY

SWEEPING MAIN STREET

ANNOYING WALL STREET

PERCOLATING BLUES JOINTS

SPILLED ON 126TH STREET

YOU BIT YOUR THUMB AT BARNARD

WHO GAVE YOU THE FINGER FIRST

NYU CALLED NEXT WITH DOTS AND LOOPS

RICH LIKE YOUR SERVICE TO

THE PEOPLE AND LOVERS

THEY DIDN'T WANT TO PUMP THE CAUSE

THEY DIDN'T NEED TO FIGHT THE LAWS

BIG STATEMENTS

SANS A GUN

SILENT PRAISE

HOLY NIGHT

ALL IS CALM

YOU LIVED LIFE

MY OWN MILITARY

I LEARNED HOW TO BE A DISTINGUISHED

ACADEMIC AND GENTLEMAN

YOU TAUGHT ME TO REMAIN CALM LIKE THE ROOTS

YOU GAVE ME DREAMS OF GLOBETROTTING

PAPERS TO READ

TEST TUBES TO MIX

IONS TO MERGE

YOU HELPED OUT OF DUTY AND OBLIGATION

BUT RARELY DESIRE

YOU WERE AN ADDICT FOR THOSE THAT BELIEVE THEY ARE WHITE

YOU WENT COLD TURKEY FOR THOSE WHO LOOKED LIKE YOU

YOU FLASHED FOR THOSE WHO KNEW YOU FROM THE OLD COUNTRY

YOU WERE DISTANT IN SPIRIT

YOU WERE LACONIC

AT TIMES, YOU WOULD LOSE THE CALM

COLLECT THE RAGE

LEAVING US WITH A DIVORCE BILL

PAYMENT STILL NEEDS PROCESSING

I TRIMMED THE SHRUBS AND HANDLED THE DIRTY WORK

SEEN AND UNACKNOWLEDGED

FOR YOU, IT WAS TOUGH BUT HEARTFELT

HARD WORK WAS A LIFETIME CREDIT FOR PRIDE

YOU TRIED TO PROCESS THE MARRIAGE CARD

BUT IT HAS EXPIRED

NO EXTENSION AVAILABLE

I LEARNED HOW TO STOP WORRYING

AND LOVE PLAYING THE BEAUTIFUL GAME

IN THE BACKYARD, ON THE ASTROTURF

THROUGH THE RAIN

CUTTING HOOSIER PRAIRIES

NOW YOU LAUGH AT MY ROMANCES

I SMILE THAT YOUR BATTLE WITH THE MILLERS

LIGHT AND REGULAR, ARE OVER

YOU WERE THE STEALTHIEST

AT TIMES BORROWING, BEGGING, AND STEALING

BUT WHEN LEAST EXPECTED

YOU ARRIVED, STANDING

WE HAVE NOT SPOKEN IN A WHILE

SINCE YOU BORROW, BEG, AND STEAL

BUT TIME SEALS A CREVICE

YOU LET US PRAY

FIVE TIMES FOR FIVE ETERNITIES

YOU DE GO WALKA NA 'TREET

YOU ASK FOR MY QUEEN

I SAY, ONE DAY, YOU GO MEET 'AM

I REMEMBER YOU VISITING

THE JERSEY WINDSOR

WITH BAGS OF CANDY

KINETIC, DOGMATIC, ELLIPTIC

IT'S YOU THAT I MIMIC

UNCONSCIOUSLY

THINGS HAPPENED

OUR TREASURY NOTES SUNK TO ZERO

ANOTHER DC AGENT

WHOSE LATE GROWTH BLED LATE EFFICIENCY

A BOOM IN COURAGE

BUSTED THE ELEPHANT

BALLOONING THE ROOM

SUMMER ICE CREAM MEMORIES

COLUMBIA ROAD TAG RUNS BACK AND FORTH

CAME FORTH AND BACK IN THE CHOCOLATE SUBURBS

SEVEN SCOOPS IN THE CONE

COOL

WE PLAYED SPORTS

WE WOULD WRESTLE

YOU ALWAYS HUNG OUT IN YOUR ROOM

OR IN THE SIDE DEN

WEIRD BUT FOLKSY

LIKE A LAND'S END SWEATER

PURE WITH CONVICTION

A LOYAL DUDE, YOU ARE

YOU WOULD ALWAYS TEST ME

REALLY THINKING THAT YOU COULD WIN

I'D GET A BUSTED LIP

YOU WOULD CRY A BUSTED YOWL

OUR BROKEN NUCLEUS BROKE YOUR SPIRIT

WHICH YOU DON'T CARE TO ADMIT

USING DIRTY WIT AS HUMOR AND PAIN

YOU BROKE ACADEMIC TRADITION

FOR ENDLESS FRATERNAL EXHIBITION

ALL THINGS END THOUGH

I CAN'T WAIT FOR YOUR NEW BEGINNING

MY OWN MILITARY

EXPENSIVE

ENDURING

VERSATILE

MANY

PROUD

ALL THINGS END THOUGH

<u>LUCK BE A DREAM TONIGHT</u>

SLEEP COMES TO EVERYONE

WIPES THE TEARS

CLEAN, NO STREAKS

SLEEP COMES TO EVERYONE

HELD BY LEFT ARMS

FAINT NECK BREATHS

SLEEP COMES TO EVERYONE

ONE SHEEP, TWO

ONE DIME, FOUR

SLEEP COMES TO EVERYONE

NEWBORNS CALM

SALES REPS PANIC

SLEEP COMES TO EVERYONE

LAKES OF MAINE

FIELDS OF KANSAS

SLEEP COMES TO EVERYONE

SWALLOWED PINOT

TYLENOL

SLEEP COMES TO EVERYONE

NO LOUD SALSA

NO GUN PISTOLS

SLEEP COMES TO EVERYONE

ANDES CLIFFS

WOOD DUTCH CLOGS

SLEEP COMES TO EVERYONE

SHADOWS YOU

SEE WHEN THERE

SLEEP COMES TO EVERYONE

ONE HALF EYELID

TWICE THE LOSS

BEACON THEATRE

BROADWAY GLOWS

MARQUEE HEAT

THE WEST SIDE

SMELLS LIKE THIS

A CUPCAKE

SOME COMTE

NICOTINE

H & H

LINEN SHEETS

OLD TALBOTS

WORN FILENE'S

THE GREENGRASS

OF BARNEY

RIVERSIDE

DOWN BY THERE

STROLLERS DODGE

HUDSON GALES

FRESH DOG SHIT

IN A DISH

FLUFFY KNISH

IN THE CAN

TRASH, IT IS

TREASURED, IT'S NOT

HAY FEVER

SWARMS THE EYES

SLOWS THE NOSE

NOT THE NAILS

OF MY HAND

OF MY MIND

HIATUS

A MAN TAKEN TO PILATE

ACCUSED OF BLASPHEMY

ENVIED BY JEWISH PRIESTS

FLAUNTED BY ELDERS

VERBAL CRUCIFIXION

PHYSICAL SCOURGE

FISTS

FEET

LEATHER

THORNS

VINEGAR

GALL

MYRRH

ROMANS

CROSS

BLACK

YELLOW CAVE MIX

THE LIFE OF A SOLDIER

DIES BUT ONCE

WALKS SOFT, CUTTING BOLDER

A BIG OLE MAN

WITH A BIG OLE GUN

EYES SCARRED BY SAND

DRY HEAT CRACKLES THE PINKIE

ARABIC SNAPS THE EAR

BEAUTIFULLY SPOKEN

ARTISTICALLY WRITTEN

IN THE BAZAARS

WITH HITS OF FABRIC

AND MISSES OF CARDAMOM

POPPED BY AN IRRESISTIBLE FORCE

DESTROYING A ONCE IMMOVABLE OBJECT

TOMORROW HITS TODAY

FOR THE IRAQIS

FOR THE AFGHANIS

AND OUR FAMILIES

THE GRASS IS GREENER

ON THIS SIDE

THE TREES ARE BIGGER

OVER HERE TOO

THE LEAVES: THE SAME

WHO ON THIS EARTH ARE WE TO BLAME?

WHEN THE STAR SPANGLED HEART PINES FOR FAME

THINGS MADE FROM CRUDE OIL

MAKE US LIVE FOREVER

AND EVER

IN THE PARK GRASS, YOUR SOFT FINGER

GRAZES MY EARLOBE

SPARKING SPIRITUAL NEURONS

GROWING THE CASTLE

THAT K FAILED TO SEE

MALCOLM WOULD BE PROUD

I HEARD A RUSTLING IN THE FOREST

I SENSED AN AIR OF UNREST

MY RADAR KNEW IT

THE WEREWOLVES SMELLED IT

BRUCE WAYNE LIVES FOR PHILANTHROPY

BATMAN SOLVES FOR CRIMINOLOGY

YOUR BODY WAS TIED IN VINE

WHILE YOUR MOUTH BIT A CLOTH, THIRSTING FOR WINE

NO FOOTPRINTS IN THE DIRT

MANY FOOTPRINTS ON YOUR SKULL

I PICKED YOU UP GENTLY

CARRIED YOU ONTO MY BACK

TO THE VALLEY OF NECTAR

WE NOURISHED OURSELVES WITH FRUIT

THEN RETURNED TO THE BAT CAVE

FACTORED WITH LABELS

OF GRACE AND JUSTICE

THOSE LABELS GREW TO GRANITE

ENTRENCHED ON THE BLUE PLANET

ONCE UNCONNECTED ON MARS

THE BAT CAVE OPENED YOUR EYES

THE METAL BARS KEPT THEM CLOSED

ALTHOUGH SOFT, THOSE BARS WERE

AN OLD ILLUSION FROM A SINKING SHIP

I CHARGED FREE SHIPPING OF LAUGHTER

SINCE I WAS BRUCE WAYNE

A GIVER

A LOVER

A THINKER

AN ENIGMA

TO HIMSELF AND OTHERS

INCLUDING YOU

YOU CHARGED ME FOR YOUR SPIRITUALITY

SWINGING BENEATH GOD'S SOCIETY

RATHER THAN WITHIN

A CONCRETE PARADISE, BELYING BABYLON

I RETURNED THE INVOICE

PAID WITH CASH, THEN BONDS

SHORT-TERM, SINCE DECISIONS ARE MADE

QUICK, IN A SUPERHERO'S TIME

ONE DAY, YOU DEFAULTED, HIDING YOUR ASSETS

I WONDERED WHY, BUT LEARNED THE REASON

YOU CHOSE A PUT OPTION

UNUSUAL FOR THAT STOCK PROFILE

PERFECT FOR A SUPERHERO

JUSTICE WAS SERVED

A RUBRIK'S CUBE ON STEROIDS

YET AGAIN, I SIT ALONE IN THE LIBRARY

YET AGAIN, I AM LOSING THE MOTIVATION

YET AGAIN, MY EYES STAY OPEN WITH FEAR

ONCE AGAIN, I AM MY OWN WORST ENEMY

WITH NO TIMING

WITH NO GRACE

I HAVE RESPECT NEAR AND FAR

YET MY PSYCHE WRESTLES IN THE MUD

OVER THE ANGLES OF LIFE

ITS CHEMISTRY

ITS PHYSICS

ITS BIOLOGY

ITS ECOSYSTEMS

ITS VAGARIES

I OBSERVE, BUT RARELY LISTEN

I ACT AT TIMES WITHOUT THOUGHT

I THINK AT TIMES WITHOUT ACTION

I CONTRADICT WITH POWER

THEREFORE, I AM SECRETLY LOST

IN SPACE RATHER THAN EARTH

I REACH OUT, TOUCHING FEW

I TAKE MORE WHILE GIVING LESS

MORE AND MORE, THOUGH

I AM SEEING

THE CLUES TO THE LAST PIECES

OF THE PUZZLE

NESTLED UNDER MY NOSE

BEYOND MY LARGE, BUSY MOUTH

ONE DAY IT WILL ALL MAKE SENSE

ONE TIME I WILL CROSS THE FINISH LINE

WITH THE CUBE OF RUBRIK

ITS BRIGHT COLORS SET IN MY HAND

ONE DAY IT WILL ALL MAKE SENSE

CENTRIFUGALS

SOLID GOLD BULLION

STREAKING FLASH GORDON

FISH DOWN IN THE CITY ATLANTIS

THROWING TULIPS AT CANDACE

MAN, LOOK AT THIS

CENTIPEDE LITURGY

NEVER FEISTY

COMBINE THESE

ADVERBS, PREDICATES, SUBJECTS

INTO PROVERBS

MADE FOR THE MANY THAT CAME

WHILE FEW ARE CHOSEN

LIKE THE JEWISH

YOU AIN'T WISHING WELL

TRYING TO KISS AND TELL

THESE VIVID FABLES

MEMORABLE LIKE AESOP

ROCKING ROUGH AND STUFF

WITH MY AFRO PUFF

LAUGHING WITH MELVIN VAN PEEBLES

SPITTING WATERMELON SEEDS

BIGGER THAN GREEK BONDS

UNFORGETTABLE LIKE BARRY

IN EVERY WAY

200 RAND

THE AFRIKANERS LIKE TO BE APART

THE BRITISH LIKE HUMAN MARTS

THE ZULU SPEARS WERE SHOT DOWN

THE XHOSA IMPUPHU, GROUNDED OUT

INDIANS SERVED TEA AND CURRY

WITHOUT CARDAMOM

TO FLAVOR THE DULLED COUNTENANCES

OF THE COLOURED

THE RAINBOW NATION ROSE

OUT OF APARTHEID RUBBLE

A FUTURE RESTS ON MANY SHOULDERS

ALONG WITH BILLIONS OF DREAMS

THE WORLD CUP OF 2010

BEGINS THE REM STAGE

AS 2010 CONTINUES THE REALITY

OF A LAND GLOWING

WITH VELDS, MOUNTAINS, AND SPRINGBOKS

OCEANS, RIVERS, AND HUTS

WEATHERED BY KNIVES, ABUSE, EPITHETS

IGNORANCE, AVARICE, AND INDIGENCE

THAT THE BIG FIVE ALONE CAN'T TAKE ALIVE

THE EAGLES NEVER LAND IN THE SAN FERNANDO VALLEY

A SHARP MOON GLOW

DUSTY PEBBLE TRAILS

WISPY MAGNOLIA TREES

HEAVY COTTON THORNS

POINTY ONES POKING AT THUMBS

THUDS FROM BOLD FOOT STRIDES

SHUDDER AT FIRST, LATER STAMP WITH PRIDE

BALDING LIKE EAGLES

TRAMPLING TULIPS FROM TUPELO

AFTER FORTY DAYS OF LASHINGS

THE CONSCIOUS MIND SOILED

THE UNCONSCIOUS MIND HAUNTED

FROM SODOMY MIXED WITH RAPE

SOAKED WITH TEETH SPIT

MALNOURISHED BLUE VEINS

A RIGHT CHEEK SLIT

OWLS MIMIC WATCHTOWERS

HARRIET TUBMAN CLIMBED THROUGH MUCH URANIUMS

SPROUTING CANADIAN TRILLIUMS

THE DISTANCE FROM THENCE IS CLEAR AND A PAST DANGER

THE JOURNEY TO LATER IS CLOUDY AND A LOTTERY WINNER

TIMELINE OF THE ELEMENTS

MATTER CANNOT BE CREATED

NOR DESTROYED

ISIS DEVELOPED COMMANDMENTS

MISCONSTRUED BY PAGANS

BUT A STRUCTURE FOR CITIZENS BEYOND

IMHOTEP DIAGNOSED THE HUMAN ANATOMY

HIPPOCRATES RECEIVED WARM FRATERNITY

ASHANTI KINGS AND EGYPTIAN PHARAOHS

LAID DOWN THE BRICKS FOR MEXICAN OLMECS

COLUMBUS AND CORTES PRETEND TO DESTROY THIS FACT

MR. WASHINGTON CARVER CREATED A PEANUT EMPIRE

MR. CARTER NEARLY BANKRUPT THIS COUNTRY

PIERRE L'ENFANT STARTED TO DRAW THE ANGLES AND DIAGONALS OF THE DIS-
TRICT

BENJAMIN BANNEKER FINISHED THE PLAN, BUT THE LIBRARY OF CONGRESS WON'T
TELL

CHARLEY PATTON PULVERIZED MOONSHINE AND HIS ACOUSTIC

ELVIS PRESLEY FORGOT TO GIVE HIM A LITTLE MORE CONVERSATION

BO DIDDLEY AND CHUCK BERRY WEAVED THE POP STANDARD

JOHN LENNON AND MICK JAGGER SHOOK THEIR HANDS

WITHOUT GREASED PALMS

CLEOPATRA IV MAINTAINED THE PTOLEMIC DYNASTY

UNTIL THE ZEALOUSNESS OF CAESAR CUT CLOSE

BABE RUTH HIT MAJESTIC SHOTS, SPAWNING TALL TALES

HIS BROAD NOSE AND FULL LIPS DESTROYED THAT MYTH FOR TY COBB

W CREATED HIS OWN WORD CRAZE

BARACK OBAMA DESTROYED THE FRACTION WITH ENDLESS NUMBER ONES

87 RAFTS FROM LUNGI

IT'S BEEN A WHILE

LONGER THAN THAT MAGNIFICENT CHICAGO MILE

WE MET AFTER A DATE WITH AMSTERDAM

FOLLOWED BY A LAM WITH CASABLANCA

THEN SAM PLAYED IT AGAIN

AT THE LUNGI AIRPORT

WITH FEMALE ROBES CALLED LAPA

MERCHANTS OF CLOTHING

PALM OIL

PEANUTS

CASSAVA LEAVES

BONGA FISH

YUCA BECOMING FUFU

SPINNING FASTER THAN A SPIDERMAN WEB

DESPITE THE OLD VICTORIAN SQUALOR

LAYING ON BENT STREET

FORGETTING KISSY ROAD

DARING NOT TO MUSS

YOUR SILKY WHITE BEACHES

YOUR CRYSTAL WATERS

I DE ASK MESEF

HOW FOR DO

I GE'FO GO TO TOUN

WHEN I FINISH ME STUDY

AHA

TECHNICAL DIFFICULTIES

ACCORDING TO YOU, I'M FUCKIN' UP

ACCORDING TO YOU, I FORGOT THANGS

ACCORDING TO YOU, I'M NOT DOWN

ACCORDING TO YOU, I SHOULD FRY

MY HAIR, MY FOOD, AND MY SEROTONIN

AND BREAK MY ENGLISH

BUT AIN'T NO REASON FOR THAT

NOT ONLY DOES NORTH AMERICA PLACE THE WELCOME MAT

AT MY FEET

MY OL' PA INVENTED IT

NOT ONLY IS MY DESTINY CLAIMED

THE WORLD IS MY OYSTER

NOT ONLY DO I REMEMBER FIVE HUNDRED YEARS

I HAVE WALKED THEM, AND AM STILL MOVING

WITH POWER STEPS AND STEALTHY VERBAL SPITS

BUT YOU THINK THE PIGS WOULDN'T DO A SEARCH

CAUSE OF MY FERRAGAMOES

YOU THINK BECAUSE I CAN'T DANCE

I'M NOT HERE AND LIVING A LIE

YOU THINK BECAUSE I'M WITH BAI, INDIRA, ROSA, AND CARMELA

I DON'T WANT LENA H.

PLEASE

IF YOU WOKE UP IN MY PORES

IN THIS COCOA EPIDERMIS

YOU WOULD BE IN A HUGGIES BOX

ON THE ISLAND OF STATEN

MUTATED

ACTING HELLA NERVOUS

SO WHAT YOU TALKIN' BOUT, WILLIS?

SOUL TAILORS

YOU TAUGHT ME ABOUT THE NIGHTSHIFT

BEFORE I COULD UNZIP MY ONEZIE

YOU CROONED THAT HEARTS OF FIRE SING LOVE'S DESIRE

YOU PERFECTED THE DUB FOR GETTING UP AND STANDING UP

YOU TOLD ME THAT BLACKS ARE AFRICANS, EVEN IN POLAND

YOU HAD THE GALL TO NOT WORRY IF HELL WAS BELOW

SINCE WE ARE ALL GOING ANYWAY

AND DO IT SUPER BAD

IN A LITTLE RED CORVETTE, GOING MUCH TOO FAST

I ASKED MY FATHER TO PLAY THIS RECORD AGAIN

DID THE FREAKS REALLY COME OUT THAT NIGHT?

SHOULD I KEEP IT AND MYSELF IN THE CLOSET?

I WON'T BE AN EXTENSION OF A BOY

BUT I CAN GET NEXT TO YOU, BABY

TEARING NOT ONLY THE ROOF OFF THIS MUTHASUCKA

BUT THAT SOUL, WIT YO HOT BUTTA

YOU TAUGHT ME ABOUT THE NIGHTSHIFT

FATHER VINCENT D'ANGELO

LOU CARNESECCA DRIBBLED FROM THE MEADOWS

TO THE GARDEN, AT 40 DEGREES BELOW

NORMAL BODY TEMPERATURE

CHRIS MULLIN'S JUMPER HIT FROM EVERY PREFECTURE

MALIK SEALY HOVERED ABOVE THE PLANKS

MARK JACKSON WAS THE DEITY OF SHIMMY

AS A NONDEITY, I CONFESSED MY EGALITARIANISM

YOUR WELCOME MAT EUTHANIZED MY UNCONSCIENCE

THE ROAD TO QUEENS WAS LONG

THE SUBWAY TO TRIBECA IS SHORTER

SIX YEARS OF DARKNESS

SUCCUMBED TO ONE BEAM OF PROMISE

YOU FORGAVE ME, FATHER

I KNOW NOW

WHAT TO DO

DU LACS

I CHEERED AND CHEERED FOR YOUR OLD GOLDEN SUIT

THE ECHOES WOKE UP MY DREAMS

MY MOTHER NOURISHED INTERNATIONAL FRUIT

LAFORTUNE CENTER GAVE OUT THE SNACKS I LOVE

SNITE FILMS SPARKED AWE LEFT BEHIND

IN THE UNLIT WALKS THROUGH JOHN ADAMS

THE STADIUM REEKED OF CATECHISMS

BEYOND THE DU LAC GEL OF BLUE

INTO THE CYTOPLASM OF MANY

THOSE VESSELS STAY FULL FOR THOSE CHOSEN

MINE FROZE AFTER ECHOES OF JOY

TWISTED INTO SHOUTS OF IGNORANCE

A QUIZZICAL GLANCE

WHEN MY HAIR FRIED BLONDE

AS GREG LEMOND RODE CEREBRAL LAPS OF LOVE AND CONFUSION

I KNOW THAT EARTH IS UNDER ME

BUT NOTRE DAME PULLED ITS RUG OUT

TO SWAT A SUPPOSED ALIEN

BIGGER THAN JEFF GOLDBLUM, BUT MORE FLY

UNHOOKED PHONICS

NOUNS GET CRUTCHES FROM A PREDICATE

ESOTERIC SUBJECTS FUNNEL INTO OBJECTS

ENTITIES THAT BUILD PARAGRAPHS ON BEECHWOOD

WOULD MINWAX COMPLETE THE SEALING

STOPPING NEWBORN CRACKS IN THE ESSAY?

BEFORE THE SENTENCES SPROUT INTO HEARSAY

YOU SAY, BUT WHAT ABOUT HERESY?

WELL, LET ME TELL YOU ABOUT HERESY

OUR OLD BUDDY, OUR OLD PAL

HE CLOAKS AS TYPED DOCTRINES ON A TYPEWRITER

A YELLOW SHEET OF PRONOUNS, PAST PARTICIPLES

PRESENT PERFECT SYLLABLES AND CONJUGATIONS

RATHER BE PERFECT FROM NOW ON THAN LATER

LATER ENDS UP IN CITY WASTEBASKETS

REUNITING WITH HIS ETERNAL CONQUEROR

YAHWEH, THE WORD SPEAKER

FIRST THE PENCE, THEN THE POUND

I COULD SAY HOW THE MIGHTY HAVE FALLEN

BUT THAT WOULD BE A FALLEN STATEMENT

CADBURY EGGS WILL NOW HAVE KRAFT CHEESE

AMERICAN SINGLE SLICES RUN MANCHESTER UNITED

CANADA SLICED OUT ITS OWN CONSTITUTION

GERMANY PLATOONED YOUR MIDSHIPMEN

INDIA BROUGHT RESTITUTION TO ITS SHORES

AFRICA WAS LEFT WITH DESTITUTION

BUT ECONOMIC RESTITUTIONS ARE COMING SOON

AUSTRALIA WORRIES ABOUT NO SOLUTIONS

NEW YEAR'S RESOLUTIONS LIVE AGAIN IN HONG KONG

SURE, THE LANGUAGE LIVES EVERYWHERE

BUT YOUR PULSE TICKS

WHILE THE EUROPEAN UNION TALKS

TO CUT THE POUND INTO A CENT

DEUCE

YOU HIT A SERVE FROM DUSSELDORF

I RETURNED IT AT THE PHILLIPS COLLECTION

YOU COLLECTED THE SHOT

LACING A FOREHAND, SKIRTING THE LINE

I ARGUED THAT BECKER HAD RETIRED

HE, THE BALL, AND BERLIN'S WALL WERE OUT

THE UMP CALLED IT A WINNER

YOU SMASHED AN ACE AT 120 KM/H

I STOOD, KICKING THE HARD COURT

CLIPPED BY DEUTSCHLAND

UNLIKE KURT RUSSELL, I ESCAPED TO NEW YORK

PLOTTING FOR THE REMATCH IN FLUSHING

YOU SERVED PROMISES

YOU VOLLEYED THREATS

WE COMPETED AGAIN ON LABOR DAY

OUTDRAWING SAMPRAS VS. AGASSI

YOU SEE MY DEVELOPED BACKHAND

WE PLAY BALLET ON THE COURT

ACES FOLLOWED BY WINNERS

BORG AND MCENROE WERE ENVIOUS

YOUR LOBS CONTINUE, COATED WITH "MEIN SUSSER!"

MY RETURNS UP THE LINE, SHOOT 'VAS?'

THE FOREHAND PUNCTUATES THE STRIPE

ICH LIEBE DICH!

I BACKHAND OVER THE NET

ICH LIEBE DICH?!

I SERVE FOR CHAMPIONSHIP POINT

I NICK THE CORNER ANGLE

GAME, SET, MATCH, SALONEUSA.

WE SHAKE HANDS AT THE NET

WHISPERING OF FUTURE DOUBLES

YOU TRAIN IN DUSSELDORF

I TRAIN WITH FORT TRYON

WE RUN THE DOUBLES CIRCUIT

OUR ELECTRICITY GENERATES FORTUNE, DOMESTIC AND GLOBAL

WEARY OF US OPEN DOMINANCE AFTER THREE TITLES

WE PUT ON NEW UNIFORMS IN GERMANY

FORMING INTO TENNIS' VOLTRON

DESTROYING FOES IN BERLIN, FRANKFURT, AND COLOGNE

BONN NOMINATES US AS SPEECH AMBASSADORS

WE PLAY A SPECIAL FRIENDLY IN AMSTERDAM

IN THE VAN GOGH MUSEUM, I CURSE

DAMN, I PULL A HAMSTRING

YOU CURSE MY VICES

I YELL ABOUT YOUR STRATEGY

OUR MINDS AND BODIES PLATEAU IN DUSSELDORF

FORESHADOWING A RETIREMENT

LATER ON, WE PLAY UNDER THE FLUSHING MOON

WE BURN DOWN BOSTON, SETTING BACK BRADY'S PLATOON

THEN OUTDUEL THE PHILLY JEWELS

NEW YORK HOLDS UP A MIRROR

WRINKLES, SORE SHOULDERS, AND BRUISED KNEES SHINE

FROM THE LONG TOUR

YOU ARE HUNGRY FOR MORE WINNERS

I AM FULL FROM SUCCESS

MY HEART NEEDS TO RECOUP RHYTHM

FOR THE NEXT TOUR

YOU RAVE ABOUT OUR PAST ADULATION

I TALK OF STOPPING FOR PRESENT MEDITATION

YOU COMPETE IN COLOGNE AT THE GERMAN OPEN

YOU FIND AN OLD FRIEND FROM TOUR AS A PARTNER

I CATCH SIGHT OF A STAR FROM OSAKA

WE MEET IN NEW YORK, GOING FOR THE GOLD

HATIANOLOGY

YOU WERE THE FIRST TO BREAK SHACKLES

DE LA CONSQUITADORS Y NAPOLEANO

YOU SHRUGGED OFF THE DEADWOODS IN OFFICE

YOU STOPPED THE GLASS BULLETS THAT JUMPED FROM BEHIND THE SHANTIES

YOU SHARE LAND, BUT NOT FRUITS, WITH DOMINICANA

YOU GAVE US BASQUIAT AND WE GOT AN ART FUTURIST

YOU GAVE US THE FUGEES, AND WE WERE NOT READY

YOU SOMEHOW, SOMEWAY, BRUSHED ARISTIDE OFF OF YOUR SHOULDER

YOU GOT BORED CLEANING UP FROM ALL THE HURRICANES

YOUR CHILDREN WENT EVERYWHERE LIKE JOHNNY CASH

THE LORD TRIED TO SHAKE YOU INTO THE GROUND

BUT YOU STOOD STILL, WITH YOUR PALM SKIRT FLOWING

YOU ARE HAITI

AN UNSTRESSED DAMSEL

LOWER SODIUM

CONAGRA TOOK OUT A COUPLE TABLESPOONS

OF TOMATO SOUP BY CAMPBELL'S

MORE TOMATO, LESS SALT

WELL, IT'S ABOUT TIME

SUDDENLY COMPANIES ARE MAKING HEALTHY CHOICES

TO HELP THEIR UNHEALTHY BALANCE SHEETS

CITIZENS STILL CAN'T BALANCE ON ONE LEG

MUCH LESS TWO FEET

FILLED WITH DIABETIC SURGES

STOPPING THE MARRIAGE OF FEET TO SIDEWALK

TO LAWNS

TENNIS COURTS

MOUNTAINS

AROUND SCHOOL TRACKS

TO FEET, THIS MOVEMENT DOES NOT TASTE GREAT

BUT YOUR BODY HAS MORE FILLING

THE DOLO

METAMORPHOSIS

TRANSCENDENTALISM

REFLECTION

WISDOM

LIGHT

EGALITARIANISM

CONNECTION

FOUR OF THEM

IN BLACK

IN RED

SYMMETRICAL

INEVITABLE

BETAMAX GALACTIC

ETERNAL

TONY SHAFRAZI

27TH STREETS ARE FAR BETWEEN

BUSTLING AT DAY

DORMANT AT DUSK

AT ONE ART LUMINARIES

EMERGING AND HISTORICAL

SPLASH CONSCIOUSNESS

AT 86 YEARS OF AGE TO 7

WITH 7 DECKS LOOPED

TO THE CACOPHONY OF

GRAND CONCOURSE, 1981

THE BOOGIE DOWN PRODUCES

SOLILOQUIES FROM KRS-ONE

VERBAL VIGNETTES BY D-NICE

PHOTO ILLUSTRATIONS ETCHED WITH THE LIPS OF LORD FINESSE

WHERE PATRONS SHALL PROCEED

THEN CONTINUE TO ROCK THE MIC

THEY WALK UP EARLY AFTER 6

CALL THE ROOM

GASP, THEN SWOON

BENSON

WHAT HAPPENED TO REAL RACISM?

BACK IN GRADE SCHOOL, THE HAZE OF CORN

BEGAN WITH QUESTIONS OF SARTORIAL MATTER

WHY DO YOU DRESS SO WELL?

WOW, YOU TALK LIKE A SENATOR FROM CAPITOL HILL!

YOU PLAY THE VIOLIN?

YOUR FAMILY LIVES IN THAT HOUSE?

YOU TAKE ALGEBRA IN THE SEVENTH GRADE?

NOWADAYS, WHITE PEOPLE SLIDE BY FASTER IN THE OFFICE

THAN THE LONG O WITHOUT SLURRING

THE 20TH CENTURY WAS SOAKED IN RACIAL TEA LEAVES

DOUBLE HELIX INTERTWINED INTO THE CRINKLED SCIATICA

OF ALL YOUTH

ERUDITE, YOUTHFUL VERNACULAR INVERTED INTO POP-CULTURE SLANGONOMICS

THAT BOARD ROOMS COLLATE INTO WHITE POWDERED JOLLY ST. NICK HEDONISM

TIES AROUND THE BLACK MAN STILL SEEM

UNUSUAL TO THE CLASSIC ANGLOPOLIS DENIZENS

UNLIKE THEIR ZEN MEMORIES

OF BENSON SERVING POT ROAST AND FLOATING SARCASM

EYES EATING UP PAC MAN PELLETS

OF VISUAL BRUTALITY

DEAR MR. MUGABE

WHY DO YOU BUY THIS EXPENSIVE SHIT IN SWITZERLAND?

THAT DRIVES PETROL UP TO 6 BUCKS A THIRD OF A LITER?

FORCING THE COLLISION OF AWKWARD DIALECTS

AND UNFRIENDLY SCORN, THE ONLY FUEL THAT DRIVES

THE MALICE, THE HEARTBREAK

THAT WASHES AWAY THE JOY FROM KILLING

CECIL RHODES, THE UNFRIENDLY, SCRAMBLING GHOST

WHO MINED THE VELDS, PUSHED OUT THE SPRINGBOKS

SWALLOWED WHOLE THE NDEBELE IDS, SHONA EGOS, AND ZULU BIRTHMARKS

ONLY CAUSE HIS PUPILS COULD NOT LET GO OF

THE GOLD GLITTER

THE GLITTER CUT DOWN RHODES

AND WILL CUT YOU DOWN TOO, MR. MUGABE

YOU FILLED YOUR MANOR WITH BENZES

AND EARNED THE PHONY RESPECT FROM YOUR BIG SISTER, ZA

ISN'T IT ENOUGH?

JUST GO TO LONDONTOWN AND DIVERSIFY YOUR PORTFOLIO

AT BARCLAYS OFF OF THE THAMES

THEN YOU CAN LEAVE THE ZIMS TO THE ZIMS

THE GAS LINES WILL GET SHORTER

BREAD WILL SPROUT AGAIN ON SUPERMARKET SHELVES

YOU WILL NOT HAVE TO BE EXILED

BY A GINZU STRIKE FROM MY MAIN MAN AND YOUR SON

NYASHA. BIG UP, PLAYBOY

CANDYMAN HAS BIG SHOULDERS

HE USED TO WHISPER THREE TIMES

CANDYMAN. CANDYMAN. CANDYMAN.

TAUNTING SHRUNKEN HEARTS WITH SHARP METAL

IN THE FOREGROUND OF A BRICK ATLANTIS

THEY CALLED IT CABRINI GREEN

BUT GRANT PARK DID NOT GIVE CABRINI ANY TREES

NOR BICYCLES NOR IPOD SHUFFLES

THEY DAMN SURE WASN'T ABOUT TO SHUFFLE NO MAGIC SILVER BEAN

PAST SOLDIER FIELD ON HALSTEAD STREET

THEY ARE STILL MAD THAT HAROLD WASHINGTON

SHOOK PAST THE CITY COUNCIL TO SHAKE THE HAND OF SWEETNESS

BETTER KNOWN AS WALTER PAYTON

HAROLD WASHINGTON, SPEAKING IN PUBLIC, IN THAT PARK

BUILDING LEGISLATIVE BRANCHES TO ENACT POSITIVE POLITICAL CAMPAIGNS

MAKING PRINCESS LAKE MICHIGAN JEALOUS

BLOWING HER LEGENDARY GALES

THAT LEAVE EARS BLUE, AND NOSES SHINING LIKE RUDOLPH

AORTA STAY WARM, GROWLING WITH ANGER

FROM DIGESTING THAT ITALIAN BEEF AFTER THAT DEEP DISH PIZZA SOUP

YEARS ARE DEEPER AND LONGER IN THE CITY OF WIND

SHORT BATS TWISTED WITH SHORTER LUCK AND FELL

LOWERING SHOULDERS OF MANY

UNTIL MICHAEL TOSSED THE BAT ONCE TO SHOOT THROUGH SIX RINGS

THEN THOSE SPIRITS GLEAMED WHITE

LIKE MARSHALL FIELDS AT CHRISTMAS

EVEN SHINING THE HUBCAPS OF MY 88 MAXIMA. DRIVEN

MODERN LIGHTS

LIGHTS BURN OUT

LIGHTS FADE AWAY

WHICH PHRASE STANDS THE TEST OF TIME?

ONLY TOMORROW CAN SAY

BUT TOMORROW CAN ONLY SPEAK

IN HUSHED TONES

OUT OF CONNECTED SPEAKERS

INTACT.

BETTER THAN BLOWN

THE LIGHT OF TOMORROW FEELS DARK

NO MATTER THE ENERGY SAVED TODAY

NO MATTER THE REACH OF YOUR FINGERTIPS

LOOSENING TO GRAZE

STRETCHING TO SLIDE

ON TO ITS PERFECT CANDLE

THAT DEFINABLE PORTRAIT

TWICE PAINTED BY RAUSCHENBERG

THIS SYMMETRICAL VISION

STENCILED ONTO A CANVAS

MATTED POLYURETHANE LIQUID COAT

MIXED INTO A FRAME

INVISIBLE TO THE SCENT

NEWLY MINTED

NIRVANA ROSE FROM MT. SAINT HELENS' WINTER DRESS

WINNING THE HEARTS OF MEN

COMPLETING SENTENCES

GIVING ANSWERS TO THE DAILY DOUBLE

TREKKING THE GLOBE

WITH SACKS OF BITTERNESS

AXES SHARPENED WITH ANGER

ANGERED THAT THE GLOBE

DRAWS ITS OWN BILE

SEVERS THE CONFUSED

INTO A SINGULAR PARTICLE

LEFT WITH TWO ATOMS

RATHER THAN FOUR

DISSOLVING THE COMPOUND

INTO A FRACTURED ELEMENT

THAT NEEDS HYDROGEN

PUDDLE SPRITZ

THROWING A FIT IN THE SKY

LEAVES CONSEQUENCES BEHIND

NOT ONLY THE 8 BALL, BUT ALSO BETWEEN THE TOES

AND OVER THE ANKLES

CUDDLING OVER THE TEXTILE FORTRESS

TURNING INTO A MOLTEN DRAWBRIDGE

WHERE HYDROGEN COMES TO DANCE

WITH OXYGEN ON THE SECOND DATE

STOPPING TO SET DATE AND TIME

BEFORE IT CONTENDS WITH SOIL

FOR NATURAL SUPREMACY

SANDBOX OF FREEDOM

THEY BOMB OUR COUNTRY

IN THE LIGHT

START OF DAY

WE'RE PARALYZED

ANTAGONIZED

THEY HAVE NO SHADES OF SHAME

GIULIANI AND PATAKI ONCE ADDED UP TO ENMITY

WHICH TENACITY THREW OUT TO THE BATTERY TERMINAL

NINE YEARS LATER WITH 9,000 CENTURY 21 BAGS

WE SIFT THROUGH SAND

TOSSING RUBBLE INTO OUR EYES

BURNING BLUEPRINTS WITH EGOS

STUFFED WITH DRY ICE

THE HORNS OF THE BULL SINK BELOW THE PATH

STABBING SAM O'NEILL

NUCLEAR FAMILIES AND DIPLOMATS

THE FDNY, NYPD, EMS. HILL STREET BLUES

LOSE BONES TO THE PORT AUTHORITY

WHO THROWS THEM TO SILVERSTEIN

WITHOUT ASKING DR. EVIL

FORGIVING THEM IS NOT DIVINE

SINCE THEY LOVE TO ERR

AS THEY FORGOT THE HUMAN

WE'RE PARALYZED

EASTERN MARKET

THE STREETS TAPPED WITH LOOTERS

AFTER DR. KING COLLAPSED

U STREET SIZZLED WITH DUKE, THEN LUCIFER

HE SENT HIS HENCHMEN FOR THE INVISIBLES

LUCIFER HAD LEAGUE CHAMPIONSHIPS

HIS TEAM EVEN BEAT THE YANKEES

HE HAD IT MADE. FAME. AN ETHIOPIAN GIRLFRIEND

A HOUSE IN NEW ZEALAND

HE MADE JERRY JONES JEALOUS

AND THAT'S HARD TO IMAGINE

OR IS IT?

THEN, ONE INVISIBLE MAN HAD VISIONS

ONES OF A TRANSPARENT METROPOLIS STILL WITH CHERRY BLOSSOMS

HE HAD A VISION OF LIFE

HE SWEPT AROUND K STREET, COLLECTING BLUE CHIPS FOR BLUEPRINTS

UNTIL HIS WHITE LIPS STAINED HIS BLUE SUIT

BEN OFFERED CHILI DOGS, SPICY ON A TOASTED BUN

HIGH RISES BEGOT HIGH TAX BRACKETS

INVISIBLE HEARTS BURN AT THE FEET OF ABE LINCOLN

FOUR SCORE AND FIVE YEARS TODAY

THE GIPPER DEFEATS BLACKNESS

FITS OF DEPRESSION SKATED IN MY VARICOSE VEINS

AFTER THE GIPPER WON A BATTLE OVER THE FROZEN CASTLES OF PRUSSIA

HE DESPERATELY PURSUED THE PUBLIC ENDEARMENT

WANTING THE GRANITE TO MELT AWAY

THAT HE HAD TO PURGE ALL THE SOUL FROM PUBLIC DISCOURSE

SOULFUL SOUP KITCHENS STOPPED SINGING A CAPELLA TUNES

TUNED OUT BY THOUGHTS OF EXTRATERRESTRIAL WONDER

CIRCLING THE RED PLANET

DILATING THE WORLD'S PUPILS SO MUCH

THAT GERMAN LIMESTONE PLAYED THE MIS-EN-SCENE OF CNN

A BEGINNING FOR A VIEWPOINT OF DILATED EXPRESSION

BREEDING THE SUFFOCATION OF CIVIL CONSCIOUSNESS

OF OLIVER NORTH TRANSACTIONS TO SADDAM

TO THE PROLIFERATION OF FOREIGN INVESTMENT

FOR THE NAZISM OF P.W. BOTHA

BOTH OF THOSE MEN GOT THEIR WISHES GRANTED

JUST BECAUSE RONALD REAGAN KNEW HOW TO ACT

AND DIRECT LIKE MR. SCORSESE

THE STEVEN SPIELBERG OF POLITICS

EVEN GOT MARGARET THATCHER TO PUT ON A HAPPY FACE

CITIZENS OF CALIFORNIA WANT HIM ON A DIME

I SAY A THREE-DOLLAR BILL

SINCE HE FELT AIDS WAS SO QUEER

GATEWAY TO THE WEST

BLACK UNEMPLOYMENT LINES STRETCH ALONG THE GREY BLOCK

PIMPLED WITH NEWPORT'S

TENSIONS CIRCLE LIKE TYCO

WESTERN LEADERS CREATED BUTS

TO MAKE US THINK ABOUT DRUGS, CHICKEN, AND CANDY

RATHER THAN LEADERSHIP LINES

LEADERSHIP RATHER COMES FROM ONES OWN PERSPECTIVE

PUSHED FORWARD WITH THE STRONG ARMS OF GOD

ALLOWING THE CHANCE TO BREAK THROUGH THE WALL OF BUTS

THAT SEPARATE THE THIN LINE BETWEEN SELF-HATE AND SELF-LOVE

THAT CEMENT OUR SUPERIOR DEPTH OF IMAGINATION

ONLY WITH VISUALIZATION OF WEALTH AND HEALTH

AND THE STEALTH PHYSICAL EXECUTION

BEGIN A LINEAR DISSOLUTION

OF THE WALLS OF BUTS

OR WHATEVER YOU CALL IT

NAP STATE

MOST DON'T BELIEVE THAT I LIVED WITH YOU

FOR EIGHTEEN YEARS WE DANCED TOGETHER

EVERY DAY, I DREAMED OF EXITING STAGE LEFT

INTERSTATE 80 WAS MY FAVORITE DESTINATION

YOU WERE SO VEXING AND TEMPTING

I HATED THAT YOU WERE ONLY AWARE OF THE RUSTY GRILL IN YOUR BACK-
YARD

I HATED THE SAME FLAT GRASSLAND DRESS THAT YOU WORE

SOMETIMES YOU DARED TO WEAR APPLE TREES ON YOUR GREEN BLOUSE

EARS OF CORN EVEN

IT KILLED ME THAT YOU ALWAYS SMILED IN MY FACE

BUT YOU HATED THAT I WAS AN AFRICAN

NOT EVEN A NIGGER, MIND YOU

BUT AN AFRICAN WEARING CALVIN KLEIN JEANS

YOU HATED THAT I COULD SPEAK AND SPELL

BETTER THAN MY TOYS

YOU HATED THAT THE FAM KICKED IT TO OUR LADY

THAT WAS YOUR GARDEN OF EDEN

PURE WITH ROMAN VANILLA EXTRACT

YOU MADE UP FOR IT SOMETIMES THOUGH

FRIENDLY FAMILIES OPEN LONG DISTANCE TABLES

TICKLED WITH FRUIT PIES, BROWNIES,

POTATOES, WITHOUT A TRACE OF ROMAINE

YOU BLEW SUMMER BREEZES THAT WHISPERED INTO MY EAR

TO PICK STRAWBERRIES AND TOAST THE SUNSET WITH A WAFFLE CONE

BUT AFTER YEARS OF BUYING MUSIC AND DRIVING ENDLESSLY

WISHING THAT YOU WOULD GO AWAY

I DID WHAT EVERY MAN TELLS HIS FIRST LOVE

FUCK OFF

BRILLIANT AND CANCELLED

I LEAP INTO THE SUBWAY DOOR SLIT

SQUEEZING MY SPINE OUT OF PLACE

THE GRADE SCHOOLERS EAT UP ORANGES

MY EYES ARE EATING UP THE SUBWAY PHOTOS

OF ANOTHER SHOW THAT ENDED EARLIER

ONLY IT WILL ALSO GET AN ENDLESS RUN OF FEARLESS SYNDICATION

TEARS SHED FOR JOY IN MY TINY ROOM

AFTER THE UNSEEN FOOTAGE AIRS

WITHOUT THE TROUBLE OF TEARING OFF THAT DVD SHRINK WRAP

HBO AND NBC WILL TAKE A COMMERCIAL BREAK

TO LAUGH AT YOU, WHITE PEOPLE OF THE WORLD

FOR LAUGHING WITH CARRIE, SAMANTHA, MONICA, AND ROSS

I AM LAUGHING TOO

BECAUSE WATCHING THE CREAMSICLE FIRE AN ORWELLIAN DRONE

WAS ONCE MUST-SEE TV

NOW IT NEEDS A CUT FROM FINAL PRO

THANKS TO THE PROTOZOA PARTY

TURTLES' FABLES

FABULOUSLY GREEN LIKE A $50 BILL

THE TURTLE GLOWED IN THE BLACK CLOUD

OF A HALLOWEEN STORM

HE HID HIS HEAD IN THE BLACKOUT OF THE OFFICE BUILDING

WHEN THE WINDS ESCAPED

BATTERY PARK AND THE FEET OF LADY LIBERTY

HE SLOWLY CLIMBED DOWN THE SOHO SIDEWALK

PASSING THE HURRIED HEEL CLICKS

OUTWITTING THE DEBT-RIDDEN COLLEGE STUDENTS

STEADYING HIS SHARP IRISES

HE KNEW THAT HE WAS SLOW TO MATCH

THE PACE OF A RABBIT

BUT HE STRODE QUICKLY

UNFOLDED HIS ELBOWS TO PLANT HIS SHELL

AND BLOSSOM ON THE BANK OF THE HUDSON RIVER

HIS BED WAS A LILY PAD, SPONGE-WORTHY

BUT HIS BED WAS NOT IN THE OCEAN

IT WAS IN THE PLAN

TAINTED GIFTS

THE BOY WALKS THROUGH THE WOODS
NOT NOTICING ANY OF HIS SURROUNDINGS
YET HE SEES THE LAKE ON HIS HORIZON
THE LAKE IS KNOWN TO BE THE DEEPEST OF ALL
ONLY A FEW DECIDE TO TRY THE FALL

MANY HAVE TOLD QUITE A TALE OF THE LAKE
HOWEVER, NOBODY WANTS TO SWIM INSIDE
FOR THE LOSS OF CONTINUITY OCCURS WITH A PLUNGE
THE BOY WONDERS AWHILE AS TO HOW
THE LAKE WILL CHANGE WITH A JUMP
HE CONTEMPLATES WITH A BACKWARD GLANCE
A SPRING OF THE LEGS BRINGS HIM UP AND ABOUT
TO THE CLOUDS, THEN DOWN INTO THE LAKE

HE FEELS AND SWIMS
OBSERVING EVERY FRAIL BIT OF SEAWEED
SOAKING IN ALL THE UNWANTED FANTASIES
THEN THE BOY RISES UP
BACK TO HIS WORLD OF CONFORMITY

SOON THEREAFTER, THE BOY WALKS ABOUT
WITH A FEELING OF BEWILDERMENT
EMPTINESS PULLS HIM OVER
TO THE LAKE AND INTO THE WATER
SPLASHING AND ENJOYING TAINTED GIFTS

INVASION OF THE STORYKILLERS

GEORGE CLINTON HAS A BRAIN

BRIGHTER THAN A ZENITH TECHNICOLOR

WHEN HE COLORED THE CITIES CHOCOLATE, AND THE SUBURBS VANILLA

THE CITY SMELLED LIKE FRESH URINE

TOO MANY BLACK PEOPLE BLEEDING ON THE CONCRETE

DEFEAT PUSHING THEIR EYEBROWS DOWN

BUT NEVER OUT OF 125TH STREET

OR BED-STUY. OR OAKLAND

OR BENTON HARBOR. OR DETROIT

OR ATLANTA. OR D.C.

OR NEW ORLEANS

HMV DARED TO SCRATCH UP THE MIX TAPE. BUT THEY GOT SCRATCHED OFF
THAT BLOCK

THAT HARLEM BLOCK

MIX TAPES ARE NOW COMPACT DISCS

COMPACT WITH HOOKS ABOUT

PLATINUM, VANDALISM, AND SECULARISM

ROMANTICISMS ABOUT THE THINGS IN THE HOOD THAT HAVE CHANGED

CHANGES IN THE FACES OF THE CROWD

FROM BLACK ON BLACK TO BLACK ON CARIBBEAN ON WHITE

ON DOMINICAN ON EUROPEAN

ADDING ITSELF TO THE TRUE TESTAMENT OF HOBBES' LEVIATHAN

THAT THE STATE HAS ABSOLUTE LEGAL POWER

TO BUILD A DISNEY STORE

FOR CHILDREN WITHOUT MEMORIES AND FLOATING BALLOONS

OF THEIR OWN SUPERHEROES

MIGHTY MOUSE, EVEN

Brighter than a Zenith Technicolor

CONFLICTED

DOUBLE STUFFED, WITH NO CREAM OF VANILLA

I WATCH EARTH ASKING BROWN TO DO IT FOR ME

BREAK CHAINS, PLANT MAIZE, SAY HEY, WILLIE MAYS

THE NEW YORK KNICKS STILL CAN'T PLAY

NEARLY 25 SPINS IN, I STILL CAN'T RECOMMEND

CALCULUS, MATHEMATICS TO YOU PHONY FANATICS

SPINNING CURRENCY ON YOUR GOLD TRIMMED ATLAS

BECAUSE WE ALL KNOW THAT AFRICA IS THE LAND

OF HUMAN MATES, READY TO RETURN THE PRIDE

BURNING WITH JUSTICE, EGALITARIAN, EXTRAORDINARILY PROLETARIAN

FROM THE PATRICE LUMUMBA LEVITATION

GRATUITY

TO BE HONEST

BEING BLACK AND GIFTED SUCKS HARD AT TIMES

WE THEN CALL MARTHA STEWART TO WHIP UP

LEMON TARTS TO SWEETEN THE LIPS

MY EFFERVESCENCE EVEN

YET THEY SAY THAT LESS IS MORE

THAT MISSED ME

MOUNT OSMIUM

POP CULTURE NEEDS BLACK INTELLECTUALS

THE WORLD BRIMS WITH 18-YEAR OLD BASKETBALL PRODIGIES

DECORATED WITH SOFT DRINKS, ARMANI PINSTRIPES, AND AFRO-EUROPEAN
WONDER

FLASHED THROUGH THE CLEAR CHANNEL VOCODER AND ESPN PLASMA

RALPH ELLISON GAVE UP, ON THE BLACK THOUGHT POOL

CALLING US INVISIBLE

MY TWO NEGLIGIBLE EYES SEE CLEARLY

THE BROTHER ON SUTTER AVENUE

PLAYING MIX TAPES OF 1986

LIVE RUN DMC WALKING THAT WAY TO YOUR EARLOBE

HEAVY VOICES SALUTING MALCOLM X

THE X FACTOR OF BLACK PSYCHOLOGY

MY EYES ALSO SEE THAT ONE WOMAN

CASCADING ON THE WEST VILLAGE COBBLESTONES

PUSHING THE STROLLER FOR LITTLE JOEY, NOT LITTLE FREDDY

BECAUSE LITTLE FREDDY NEEDS MONEY FOR HIS SCHOOL FIELD TRIP

TO THE BROOKLYN MUSEUM OF ART

WHERE ZULU SPEARS, ASHANTI BRICKS, AND EGYPTIAN HIEROGLYPHICS

ANSWER THOSE QUESTIONS, FROM A THREE SEAT LEATHER SOFA

AN ECLIPSE

LIVE FROM THE HUDSON HOTEL

DRAPED IN ORNATE GLAMOUR

YOU BEAMED WITH MODERNITY

CURIOUS, I SPOKE OF EARTH, WIND, AND FIRE

YOU YELLED, "MARVIN GAYE!"

I LAUGHED, FILLED WITH EXCITEMENT

YOU WERE THE SUNRISE, MY CHANCE AT REDEMPTION

AFTER FALLING SUDDENLY IN A KOREAN BATTLE

UNSEEN BY MY NEURONS

THEN YOU SET IN THE FAR EAST FROM WHENCE YOU ROSE

I SPUN FROM THE HEIGHTS TO QUEENS, THROUGH BROOKLYN AND THE SOUTH

TO CLEANSE IN MIAMI SALTWATER

I MEMORIZED YOUR LAUGHS, YOUR SMILES, AND YOUR WHISPERS

SEPTEMBER, YOU ROSE AT HALF SET

ONLY TO FADE SLOWLY IN OCTOBER

I RAN THROUGH THE LOWER EAST SIDE

VIEWING YOUR SUNSPOTS WITH A TELESCOPE

I RAN TO PHILLY AND RECRUITED MAXWELL

PLANNING A NEW ERA

BUT THE BATTLE HAD BEEN LOST

WAY BACK IN JULY

WHEN YOUR RAYS FRIED MY SKULL

AND GRACE BOILED MY SOUL

INTO BROCCOLI

ALL WORN OUT

FELLED

PLANNING A NEW ERA

KNOWLEDGE WAS POWER

TO ENLIGHTEN IS NOT TO DWELL

BUT TO INFLATE THE MASSES, FROM MASSACHUSETTS

INTO THE WILD OF MYANMAR

WILD NIGHTS IN TRIBECA

ARE KILLING MY BRAIN

WHISPERING TAUNTS AND ILLUSIONS

OF GRANDEUR, STEAMED WITH MUSSELS AND LIP GLOSS

STAINING MY SHIRT AND CHEST

BEFORE, MY VENTRICLES BEATED

THE WORDS OF MALCOLM

WHO YELLED THROUGH BALDWIN

WHO SWEATED WITH ELLISON

WHO ATE WITH REED

WHO RAPPED WITH NEWTON

WHO STRATEGIZED WITH SEALE

WHO LAUGHED WITH DAVIS

WHO COUNSELED WITH HAMPTON

WHO SPARKED FANON

WHO INSPIRED BIKO

WHO BUILT MANDELA

WHO WARNED NKRUMAH

WHO THEN TOLD RAWLINGS

TO WATCH CHARLES TAYLOR

SO THAT HE WOULD KEEP SIERRA LEONE

OFF HIS NAILS, OUT OF HIS CLUTCHES

NOW I WALK THE CITY

UNSURE OF GRABBING THE TORCH

FOR SHAME

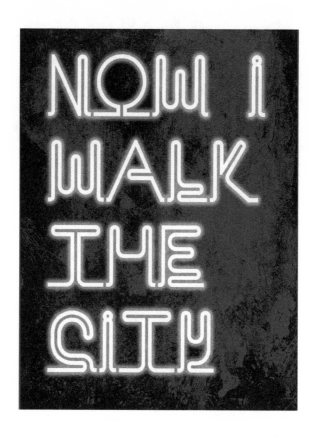

THE SHOW

YOU ARE A BENCH COACH AT THE SINGLE-A LEVEL

A ROLE THAT HAS PURPOSE

FOR ONLY THAT SITUATION

IT BUILDS LOCAL FERVOR, THEN GLOBAL SILENCE

I'M BATTING .320 AT DOUBLE-A

PLAYING A GRACEFUL CENTERFIELD

FOR THE LOVE OF SUN, GRASS, PEANUTS

THE CAMARADERIE FROM FANS

THE TEAM HISTORY

THE PRIDE OF MY UNIFORM

NEXT SEASON IS A SHORT STOP AT TRIPLE-A

THEN AN ITALIAN TOURNAMENT

THE SPEEDS CHANGE WHEN THROWN FROM THE MOUND

MY DETERMINATION STAYS THE SAME

I SWING SOFTLY AND HIT HARD

BECAUSE THE BRIGHT LIGHTS BECKON

CONSTANT DRIZZLE

I KNOW THAT YOU'RE GONE

I KNOW THAT IT IS OVER

BUT MY EYEBROWS COLLECT RAINDROPS

SPITTING SLEEPLESSLY IN SEATTLE

THEY FLOAT WITHOUT GRAVITY

WHILE PENETRATING WITH PERMANENCE

OF A MICROFICHE ERA

THAT NEVER TRANSFERRED TO BLU-RAY

DESPITE OUR VIVID COLOR SPECTRUM

WE GLOWED LIKE STARS FROM THE GILDED AGE

AS OUR RELATIONSHIP FLICKERED DUST, ASH, AND EMBERS

I TRIED TO DOUSE MY FLAMES WITH CALM

AND REPLACE THEM WITH SMILES OF SUNSHINE

BUT CAMEL LIGHTS STAINED MY TEETH

THAT PRETEND TO SALVE MY RUINS

I KNOW THAT YOU THINK LITTLE OF ME THESE DAYS

PERHAPS WONDERING WHY IT EVER STARTED

WHILE I CHATTER TEETH IN THE GREAT LAKES

UNDER BLACK CUMULUS CLOUDS

TWO WINDOWS

I LOOK THROUGH TWO WINDOWS AGAIN

WITH TWO EYES RATHER THAN FOUR

LOOKING AT THE SIDEWALK ALONE

RATHER THAN THE CONSTELLATIONS TOGETHER

I CAN FIND ORION AND SAGITTARIUS

WITH SOMEONE

I CAN FIND THEM ALONE

I WILL FIND FISCAL GUIDANCE ALONE

I WILL BETTER RESPECT PERSONAL BOUNDARIES ALONE

THEN I WILL FIND AN EMPRESS AGAIN

OUTSIDE OF THESE PANES

THE OLD DAYS

MYSTICS FROM THE FAR EAST NOW CALCULATE P/E RATIOS

MYSTICS FROM THE FAR EAST MEASURE TAXES ON TEA

NOMADS FROM THE SUBCONTINENT PLAY THE FLUTE

BEFORE INSTALLING A NETWORK

GANDHI SMILES FROM ABOVE, SEEING HIS SALT REVOLUTION

TAKE A DIGITAL REPRISE

THE BICEPS OF PUTIN FLEX WITH THE SCOWL OF LENIN AND STALIN

THE KREMLIN SPREADS OIL FROM THE SIBERIAN TUNDRA TO ST. PETERSBURG
CASTLES

OZ BOUNCES ON THE RED PLATEAU

AND STOPS THE TASMANIAN DEVIL

THE MOTHERLAND LIVES WITH PERSISTENT DEMONS

SMILING TO GIVE RHYTHM, JOY, HARVEST, AND WISDOM

THE RAINFOREST GROWS WITH VIVID COLORS AND OLYMPIC PRIDE

RONALDO KICKS STONES THROUGH THE SLUMS, ROBBING FEAR FROM THE HOOD

PILGRIMS AND COLONISTS BITE THEIR THUMBS

WORRIED THAT A SEQUEL TO ROME IS IN PRODUCTION

NO OPTIONS

MR. BILL MEETS WITH MRS. INSPIRATION

HE IS KNIGHTED TO SAVE WHITE BLOOD CELLS

HE NEEDS TO RESCUE DRYING BONES

AND ENERGIZE FRAYING MUSCLES

HE GOES TO WASHINGTON

TO TRIUMPH LIKE MR. SMITH

HIS STAFF IS SHARPENED

WITH WORDS DRAWN BY A MIGHTY PEN

HE CUTS THROUGH THE HOUSE

BLOODIED, BUT STAYING STRONG

THE BLOOD KEEPS FLOWING INSTEAD

ON THE WAY TO THE SENATE FORTRESS

THEY TAKE HIS LIVER AND FRY IT

A PROUD KNIGHT THEN

A JESTER NOW

NIKE AIR PEGASUS

THEY CALL IT A STRETCH RUN

ALTHOUGH IF YOU STRETCH TOO FAR

YOU CAN PULL SOMETHING

RUNNING FOR TOO LONG

CAN TAKE YOU OFF TRACK

THUS, THE BEAUTY OF THE STRETCH RUN

WHERE YOU RUN TO STRETCH YOUR PACE

ACQUIRED WITH A STENCH IN TASTE

SETTLES THE PACE IN WHICH YOU STRIDE

RIGHT FROM THE SHOE STORE AS A CHILD

INTO THE VISIONS OF GRANDEUR

WHICH ONCE MOVED IN YOUR OWN MIND

AT FRANTIC PACES

NOW AFTER A STRETCH RUN

YOU STRETCH THE NYLON BAND

OF ONE PART TO A SNAP

THEN YOU GLIDE

YOUR INELASTIC STRIDE

FLIES ON THE EARTH

YOUR STEPS HOVER

ABOVE THE FOXES AND HOUNDS

THESE CUSHIONED NEOPRENE SOLES

CRUSH THE ROCK MARRIAGES

LEFT AND RIGHT

BACK AND FORTH

UP AND DOWN

DIP AND DRIVE

OUT THAT LIFE

YOUR STEPS HOVER ABOVE THE FOXES AND HOUNDS

DISCO FAME

GREATNESS ILLUMINATES ABOVE AND BELOW

GREATNESS BRINGS FREE GIFTS

MATERIAL, SOMETIMES CELESTIAL

GREATNESS STREAMS PAGE VIEWS

GREATNESS COLLECTS HIGHER BOUNCE RATES

GREATNESS IS LONELY

GREATNESS ISOLATES THE MIND

GREATNESS STRENGTHENS THE SPIRIT

GREATNESS CUTS BETWEEN CONNECTIONS

GREATNESS NOURISHES DESIRE

GREATNESS CAN LAST FOR QUITE AWHILE

GREATNESS, IN ONE SENSE, CONCLUDES

GREATNESS, IN ANOTHER, REFLECTS

GREATNESS COVERS OUR WOUNDS

GREATNESS OPENS THEM FARTHER WHEN CRACKED

YOU ARE GREAT BECAUSE YOU LIVE TO PUT IN WORK

STREET KNOWLEDGE, ACADEME, COURAGE, AND WISDOM BREED GREAT INSIGHT

YOU SMELL GREATNESS IN THAT PARFUM DE COEUR

YOU LISTEN FOR GREATNESS IN YOUR INSTRUCTION

YOU FEEL GREATNESS IN THE BUILDING

YOU SEE GREATNESS IN YOUR GENETICS

YOU TASTE GREATNESS IN YOUR HOMEMADE BLUEBERRY MUFFIN

YOU BUILD FOR GREATNESS IN YOUR COMMUNITY CENTER

I FEEL GREAT JUST TO EXIST

IT'S JUST LIKE A DREAM

FORTY-FOUR HERBS AND SPICES

CONCH

TAMARINDS

FUFU

YUCA

PEPPER SOUP

BANANA CAKES

JOLLOF RICE

COCONUT

PIG'S FEET

CANDIED YAM

TURNIPS

ROASTED CHICKEN

BLACK EYED PEAS

CRACKLING PORK

SWEET CABBAGE

CASSAVA LEAF

WHOLE POTATOES

MUSTARD GREENS

BLUEFISH

DIASPORA MENU

A HARVEST FOR THE PEOPLE

FINGERS LICKED AROUND THE WORLD

SOUL FOOD

SOUL POWER

A TEST TUBE, WITH LOVE

ROMANCE

THE MATCH THAT MEETS A DROP OF OIL

STILLNESS THEN, A FLAME A FLUTTER NOW

GOBS OF AMBER

STREAMS OF MAGMA

THAT DASH BY YOUR EYEBROW

HEIGHTEN YOUR VEINS

DIZZY IN THE JAR

ONE OF CLAY

IN A HUMAN BIOSPHERE

EXPERIMENTS THAT BUBBLE

PUNCHING THE TEST TUBE

THEN SPLASHED ON THE FLOOR

ROMANCING THE STONES

THROWN AT YOUR HEART

TO THREATEN THE PORCELAIN DREAM

BUT DISSOLVE IN AIR

LIKE A VIRGIN

TOUCHED FOR THE FIRST TIME

SO VERY MUCH AT ONCE

THEN SILENCE HUGGED US BOTH

THEN THE BELL RINGS

WE BREAK FOR CANDY

THE CONVERSATION

LIKE ALL ELSE IN OUR ERA

IT BEGAN WITH A TWEET FEED

SPRUNG FROM A TELEVISION PROGRAM

SHOWN ON ESPN

THAT I REMEMBER SEEING LIVE

BACK IN THE EARLY 1990S

WHEN ALL THE BLACK KIDS

SAT TOGETHER IN THE CAFETERIA

THE FAB FIVE WORE THE MAIZE AND BLUE

A COLOR SCHEME I WAS RAISED

TO LOATHE

AS THE GOLDEN DOME GLOWED

THROUGH MY BEDROOM WINDOWS

GLISTENING MY PLAN

JALEN ROSE SAID SOMETHING THEN

PLAYED LATELY

THAT STILL STINGS TODAY

THE HILLS BRED

A MAN NAMED GRANT HOUSE

SMART IS WHITE

BALLIN' IS KING

IN THE HOOD

IN THE FIELD

ON THE BLACKTOP

WE TALKED VIRALLY

WIRES UNTAPPED

UNLIKE GENE HACKMAN

WE ASKED ONE ANOTHER

WHO MADE THAT RULE?

MARCUS GARVEY WAS SMART

CORETTA SCOTT KING STUDIED WOODWINDS

GEORGE WASHINGTON CARVER WAS LEONARDO DA VINCI

OUR FATHER COULD BUILD

CHEMICAL FORMULAS

ORGANIC TO GASEOUS

JAWANZA KUNJUFU SCOPED

THE PAVEMENT OF THE SOUTH SIDE

HE KNEW THE BELL WASN'T RINGING IN SCHOOL

ANYHOW, MY BROTHER UNDERSTOOD

MY TENSIONS

WITH OUR EDUCATORS

WITH THE CORNFIELDS

WITH THE BUNGALOWS

I NO LONGER NEEDED MR. CLEAN

TO SHINE ON

THAT WE HEARD LIES FOREVER

BUT FELT TRUTHS IN EVERY BREATH

THAT TREATMENT

I SIT AND WONDER WHAT IT ALL MEANS

WE DANCED IN AND OUT OF EACH OTHER'S IRISES

DUE TO CONSEQUENCES BEYOND OUR CONTROL

ONE MINUTE, WE'RE HERE

THE NEXT STEP, WE'RE THERE

WE WADE THROUGH TENSION

WITH OUR HIPS

SWINGING FOR THE FENCES

SHAKING FROM THE TREBLE

WE DON'T KNOW WHAT TIME IT IS

FOR EITHER OF US

WE DON'T KNOW WHO'S KEEPING TRACK

BUT BACK TO THE LECTURE AT HAND

PERCEPTIONS ARE PERFECTED FOR ALL THOSE WHO UNDERSTAND

THAT DRIVING BY NIGHT

BREEDS AN ILLUSION

MISSING SHADOWS

FRESH WATERMELON RINDS

A SUMMERTIME DANCE

PLAN TO WORK

WORK TO PLAN

A CONSONANT AT ONCE

A VOWEL WITH OTHERS

MANY THOUGHTS TRAVEL

ONE THOUGHT STAYS HOME

OTHER IDEAS LIGHT UP

SOME IDEAS DIM AWAY

RARELY BURNING OUT

IN THE CONSTANT SPIN OF OUR AXIS

UNFELT BY YOUR FEET

UNSEEN THROUGH YOUR EYES

AS WE BUILD TODAY

WITH THE HANDS THAT TIE

CALLUS THE HANDS THAT BREAK

AS WE PAINT TODAY

WIND THE BRUSH STROKES DRIED ON CANVAS

AS WE WRITE TODAY

STENCIL INK STAINED TO A BOOK

AS WE SLAB A LAYER OF GLUE

PRESS ONE BRICK AT A TIME

EVERY LEGO BRICK IN THE PLAY ROOM

I'M WALKING AROUND

I GET THEM

RED BLOCKS

GREEN TIPS

FAT PIECES

I'M PICKING UP

I STACK THEM

I PUSH THEM ON

I FIT THEM

THEY'RE MINE

I BUILD THEM

THEY'RE MINE

I FORM THEM

A WINDOW IN

IT SWINGS OUT

ONE FLOWER UP

A LILAC

IT GROWS

I SPREAD IT

IT GROWS

I FEED IT

LEFT PENDULUM, RIGHT CLICK

TICK TOCK

THE GRANDFATHER CLOCK

CLOCKWISE

COUNTERCLOCKWISE

ONE OBSERVATION

A VALUE JUDGMENT

A BASIC OPINION

EMOTIONAL SLANDER

STICKING TO MY GUNS

UNDOING A BOND

CLEAR INJUSTICE

A STRONG VOICE

UNCONTROLLED NEUROSES

OVERT SMILES

COVERT DISS

IRISES LEFT, IRISES RIGHT

BROW STRAIGHT, CHIN UP

DESIRE EVEN

RECEPTION SCATTERSHOT

VERTIGO

DRAINED, THOUGH

JAMAICA-VAN WYCK

YO....IT'S MAD DARK IN HERE..

WHY DOES IT SMELL LIKE OLD NAILS?

OH SHIT, I PASSED OUT!

HEY, HELLO

THE PLACE WHERE I DWELL.

TELLS MANY SHORT TALES.

ABOUT BEING A FOOL IN LOVE.

I APPLIED TO YOUR LAW SCHOOL.

BY THE COURT APPELLATES. 2002.

GOT WAIT-LISTED. THEN DENIED.

I WALKED ON FULTON STREET, THROUGH THE MALL.

MY CAMPUS VISIT FELT RIGHT.

THEN I MOVED TO THE ROTTEN APPLE.

I DID A LAYOVER IN QUEENSBORO.

I HIT THE GREAT NORTH.

UPTOWN.

THE HEIGHTS. THE BACHATA IN YOUR EARDRUM.

PIERCING YOUR DOME.

FOR THE REST OF YOUR LIFE.

THE BRONX. STAYING GROWN.

HARLEM, NY. YOU ALREADY KNOW.

I STILL WANTED MY MODEL WIFE, THOUGH.

I GOT STAR STRUCK IN THE 90S.

WALKING THE STREETS OF DOWNTOWN. THE VILLAGE. THE LES.

TRIBECA. SOHO. CHINATOWN.

THE PUNKS. THE BUMS. THE SOUP KITCHENS. THE DOOWOP GROUPS.

THE SARTORIAL MAVENS.

THE RAPPERS.

THE BEAT BOX MAGICIANS.

THE NIKES.

THEN THEY MOVED AWAY. THEY STARTED ROLLING WITH YOU.

I STARTED FLIRTING WITH YOU.

CROWN HEIGHTS.

EAST NEW YORK.

CANARSIE.

FORT GREENE.

WILLIAMSBURG. BUSHWICK.

SUNDAYS WITH MY FAM IN BED STUY.

CONEY ISLAND FUNNEL CAKES.

CLINTON HILL, WHEN IT WAS THE FINEST CHOCOLATE.

SUNSET PARK BAKERIES.

RED HOOK PUPUSAS.

I EVEN RODE UNDERNEATH THE VERRAZANO.

A BICYCLE, SOLD TO ME BY A RUSSIAN AUCTIONEER.

SHEARING AT SHEEPSHEAD BAY.

THE SALT DUSTED MY EYEBROWS.

I LEFT, BUT ALWAYS CAME AROUND.

IN THE SUMMER.

IN THE SPRING.

I WALKED THE PROMENADE WITH GIRLFRIENDS.

I WORKED AT YOUR FIRMS BY THE BRIDGE.

YOU EVEN ROMANCED BASKETBALL AWAY FROM NEW JERSEY.

NOT THAT THEY NOTICED.

OR CARED.

THEN YOU KEPT TORTURING ME.

WEEKENDS ON GRAND STREET.

BUILDING WITH CREATIVES.

FINE.

YOU HAD ME AT HELLO.

IT'S GOOD TO SEE YOU.

BEACONATORS

ASSATA

AMADOU

TRAYVON

DARIUS

BELL

LOUIMA

CHIN

OSCAR

RODNEY

ANTRON

RICHARDSON

SANTANA

WISE

YUSUF

DANE

ALAN

KIMANI

DIAZ

DIGGLES

ALEXANDER

SHAKUR

EMMETT

LOPEZ RIVERA

ALBERTA

BAEZ

BLAND

CHAPMAN

SCOTT

RICE

CLARK

HURD

JACKSON

TSUCHIDA

OLMOS

ANDERSON

SMITH

CAREY

PHILANDO

BOYD

GARNER

MCKENNA

BROWN

HERNANDEZ

MCDONALD

SIMON SAYS....WALKONTHESTREET

SIMON SAYS....STANDUPANDSITSTRAIGHT

SIMON SAYS....PULLUPYOURPANTS

SIMON SAYS....LOOKINMYEYESWHENITALKTOYOU

SIMON SAYS....ENOUGH!!!!!

BLANK RELATIONS

THEY WANT ME THERE

AT THEIR STIFF, DREARY GATHERINGS

THEY ARE DYING TO ASK ME STUPID QUESTIONS

ABOUT MY HAIR STYLES

ABOUT MY FABRICS

THEY CONTINUE TO FUCK UP WHEN PRONOUNCING MY NAME

EVEN WHEN I SPELL IT CORRECTLY FOR THEM

IN LINGUAL PHONICS

THEY TRY TO MOCK MY DIALOGUE

AS THEIR UNDERWEAR SOAKS

THEY TRY TO SAY THAT I'M NOT THE REAL THING

WHEN THEY WOULD NEVER WALK ON THE BLOCKS THAT I HAVE

WHEN THEY HAVE NEVER HELPED THE PEOPLE THAT I HAVE

IN THE BUILDINGS

OF THOSE BLOCKS

AT THESE HOUSES THAT I HAVE

THEY WOULDN'T BE CAUGHT DEAD IN THE TOWNSHIPS I'VE SEEN

THEY WOULDN'T BUY GOODS AT THE BAZAARS I'VE HEARD

THEY KNOW THAT THEY ARE FLUNKIES

AT THIS TECHNICOLOR GAME

SO THEY WANT ME TO HELP THEM ACE

THE GUILT TEST

BECAUSE IN THEIR BUBBLES

I CAN'T EXIST IN PURE FORM

OTHERWISE THEIR HEADS WOULD POP

THEY THEN WOULDN'T MATTER

THEY COULDN'T DESTROY OR INFECT

EVERYTHING THAT THEY TOUCH

WHICH TURNS TO STONE LIKE MEDUSA

OR EVIL, LIKE ORSON WELLES

OH WELL

I CAN'T EXIST IN PURE FORM

GARDEN STATION

I HAD BEEN RIDING DOWN THE INTERSTATE

IN A BUS WITH FLIMSY COOL AIR

THOUGHTS SKATE ON THE CEREBRAL CORTEX

TALKING LOUD AND SAYING NOTHING

THEY ECHOED THE STILL WAVE OF THE MEADOW

A WIND THAT LAIRD HAMILTON MAY PUSH THROUGH

BUT THAT STILL FADES TO GREY

THESE TIMES STILL WADE AWAY

THE YELLOW PAINT STAYS TODAY

THE DRIVER SAYS LITTLE ON THE MIC

NOT CENTER STAGE

PASSENGERS SAY A LOT

NOT KNOWING THAT THE BATHROOM DOOR DOESN'T CLOSE

NOT KNOWING THAT SOAP IS AN ENDANGERED SPECIES

OUR LOSS; GERMS' GAIN

THIS IS SUPPOSED TO BE WHEN

MOTHER SUPERIOR JUMPS THE GUN

BUT SHE BARELY LIFTED A TOE

ABOUT WHICH TRICK TO PLAY ON US

A BOLT OF LIGHTNING

A BUCKET OF NOVEMBER RAIN

COLD DROPS DIVING FROM THE CHIN

CRACKED ON THAT STONE GROUND

JURISPRUDENCE

IF IT DON'T FIT, YOU MUST ACQUIT

BUT DO YOU QUIT BEFORE THE MOVE?

DO YOU QUIT BEFORE THE OPPORTUNITY?

TO STOP, LOOK, AND LISTEN

FOR THE CHANCE TO ROLL?

OR DO YOU REFUSE TO START STOPPING?

DO YOU REFUSE TO LOSE?

DO YOU REFUSE TO SETTLE THOSE EYELIDS

ON A STONE WHICH GATHERED MOSS

EVEN THOUGH MOSS JUST FITS GOOD

ON THE FACE OF A STONE

THIS IS WHY MOSS AND STONES ARE NOT ACQUITTED

THEY DO FIT

THEY DO DETERMINE THE SPOT

THEY TAKE A STEP OFF OF THE ROAD

GOING TO THE BRIDGE

THE BRIDGE THAT TOWERS

THE BRIDGE THAT JUMPS

THE RIVER OF DEFEAT

THE LAKE OF FIRE

BUBBLES INTO THE VELD

ARE YOU LISTENING?

HITCHCOCK AND THEM

THE BIRD IS THE WORD

ONE IN THE HAND, TWO IN THE BUSH

BEATS GEORGE EVERY TIME

FLASH.EYEBROWS.SPAN

THE WOMEN

THE WOMEN

THE GIRLS

THE GIRLS

THE WOMEN

THE WOMEN

THE GIRLS

THE GIRLS

THE ONES

THE ONES

THE LOVERS

THE LOVERS

THINKING OF THAT

DREAMING OF THIS

ALWAYS............FOREVER

THE MAKERS

THE TAKERS

OF HOME

OF MOVES

THEY WATCH

THEY TELL

THEY WARM

THE SPACE

THE BUILDERS

THE TILLERS

OF SPACE

OF SOIL

THEY PLANT

THEY SOW

THE WORKERS

THE DEALERS

THE DEALERS

THE WORKERS

THEY VOTE

FOR CAUSE

THEY BRING

THE PEACE

THEY START

THE FIGHT

THEY SCRAP

THEN CLAW

THEY LAUGH

THEY SMACK

YOUR ARMS

YOUR ASS

THAT'S RIGHT

LIGHTS OUT

NEW ERA CAPS

WE ARE BORN TO LIVE

A PENNY FOR YOUR NEW THOUGHTS

THE RESERVES OF ALL TIME

TOBACCO HAZE

CRYING FOR THE BELOVED COUNTRY

ONE WHERE MATTERS ARE MADE UNCLEAN

WITH CIVIL BLOOD SHED IN DREAMS

WHERE CIVIL HANDS ARE STRUCK IN DAYLIGHT

SAVING TIME FOR NOBODY

LOSING CIVIL SPIRITS MADE FOR YOU

I WANTED TO TOUCH YOUR EVILS

I WANTED TO SLOW YOUR STRESS

I WANTED TO BITE YOUR WOUNDS

PRESSING YOUR SORES

PULLING YOUR KNOTS

EVEN NIBBLE YOUR CORNS

THAT ITCH TO A QUIBBLE

BUT NOT LIKE ITCHING YOUR ACHILLES

A TENDON FOR THAT TENSION

THE TENDONS THAT BIND THE HEART

ONE THAT DUSTS THE MOUNTAINS WITH SNOW

CAPPED ON THE TOP AND BOTTOM

OPENING FIELDS FOR THE GROWTH OF OXYGEN

THE BLOOM OF VIOLETS

THE BLEND OF CARAMEL AND COCOA

POURED OVER ICE

TOP

YOU WIND ME UP

SPIN

SPIN

SPIN THE GREY CIRCLE

I COLLECT RINGS

BLUE

BLACK

TEETERING A LITTLE

NO FALLING DOWN

RED

WHITE

TEETERING A PLENTY

SILVER HALOS

GREEN

BROWN

WINDING RIGHT A LITTLE

A ROUND SHADOW COIN

CLOCK

WISE

COUNTER IT, I DARE YOU

NAILS

A SMOOTH ALDER SPROUTS IN ROCK CREEK PARK

THE DOGWOOD SPRINGS FOR INWOOD HILL

THE SYCAMORE MAPLE TREE CURVES ON FORT TRYON PARK

THE RED FLARES RISE OUT OF CENTRAL PARK

PRAIRIE GRASS GROWS AT POTATO CREEK

ASHES TO ASHES, DUST TO DUST

MIND OVER MATTER

ALTHOUGH DR. SEUSS SAID

THAT THOSE WHO MATTER DON'T MIND

AND THAT THOSE WHO MIND DON'T MATTER

IT MATTERED TO ODYSSEUS

WHO USED HIS BRAINS TO TRICK

THE BRAWN OF CYCLOPES

BUT HE USED HIS BRAWN

TO BUY TIME FOR HIS BRAIN

TO DIRECT TO CYCLOPES, THE BRAWN SCULPTURE

A BRAIN FREEZE, CRACKING HIS SKULL

SO ODYSSEUS SHOWED

THAT ONE GETS GOT WITH BRAINS AND BRAWN OVER BRAWN

THINK ABOUT THAT

MADE WITH BASF

THE REVOLUTION WAS NOT TELEVISED

YOUR FATHER TOOK OFF THE TV KNOBS WHEN YOU GOT IN TROUBLE AT SCHOOL

THE REVOLUTION WILL NOT BE TELEVISED

IT WILL BE HASHED AND TAGGED TO DEATH ON TWITTER

IT WILL BE CONNECTED, WITHOUT THOSE LOST IN A VIRTUAL REALITY OF IGNO-

RANCE AND FEAR AND COWARDICE

IT WILL BE CHARGED BY THOSE WHO FORGOT THEIR IPHONE CORD AT HOME

BECAUSE THEY ARE OUT FIGHTING GERRYMANDER LAWS

IT WILL DISSOLVE OLD BODY CELLS IN BATH WATER

IT WILL FRACTURE BONES MADE WITH CALCIUM

IT WILL PUNCTURE WORN LUMBAR NERVES

IT WILL EDUCATE THOSE BEGINNING TO UNDERSTAND

IT WILL ENLIGHTEN, THOSE ON THE GROUND, IN THE COURTS

IT WILL INSPIRE, YOUR FOREFATHERS AND GRANDMOTHERS

IT WILL BUBBLE TO THE SURFACE

SPILLING OVER THE LIPS OF YOUR CHEMICAL BEAKER

EXPLODING INTO THE SKY

FALLING TO THE SOIL, FRESHENING THE AIR

A SIGHT ADVANCE

TO THINK IS TO SIGNIFY EXISTENCE

TO IMAGINE IS TO GROW A LANDSCAPE

TO DREAM IS TO SHADE IN THE FIGURES

8 OF THEM. BECAUSE THAT IS ENOUGH

TO PONDER IS TO LOOK IN THE POOL'S TOP SKIN

TO SCRUTINIZE IS TO CHISEL

THEN WE LOOK FORWARD

THROUGH THE BROKEN BOULDERS

WITH TWO EYES, NOT JAUNDICED

A THIRD ONE WITH SEDIMENTS OF CRUST

WE SHOUT, "PALANTE"!

BECAUSE OUR PUERTO RICAN PEOPLES TOLD US TO DO THAT

WE MARCH FORWARD BECAUSE OUR LEGS DON'T GRACEFULLY WALK BACKWARD

WE WADDLE FORWARD. SLOW AND STEADY

NOT TO WIN ANYTHING

MIND YOU

SINCE WINNING ANYTHING

IS LITTLE MORE THAN SOCIAL PROPHECIES

PROVIDING SPIRITS THAT TINGLE

RATHER THAN THE BULB OF HEDONISM

SEE, HEDONISM POWERS A BULB

NOT OUT OF NECESSITY

BUT RATHER OUT OF CONTEXT

WE USE PHYSICAL OBJECTS OF MATTER

TO ILLUMINATE TRUTHS EVIDENT

IN YOUR TASTE BUDS.

OUT OF YOUR PHALANGES.

FROM THAT AORTA.

WITHOUT A SWITCH.

MOVING THROUGH AN OCEAN WAVE.

ON A CASH ADVANCE

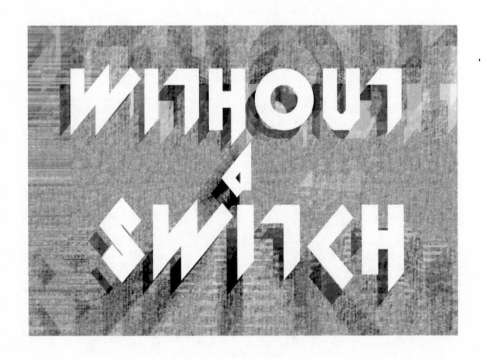

<u>YOU SHOWED ME</u>

BLACK CHAOS

BLACK HANDS

BLACK STEEL

WHITE FEAR

WHITE GAS

WHITE LIES

BLACK FISTS

BLACK POWER

WHITE ROCKETS

WHITE WEAPONS

BLACK SPIRIT

BLACK TAR

WHITE BADGES

BLACK SIGNS

BLACK JORDANS

WHITE CHAINS

BLACK TWITTER

FOX NEWS

WHITE DENIAL

SLAVE STATE

BLACK TOWN

FREE STATE

WHITE COUNSEL

BLACK

BLACK AND BROWN

BLACK

BLACK AND BLUE

WHITE HORNS

GREY DOGS

BLACK STICKS

WHITE CARS

WHITE LIGHTS

BLACKED OUT

WHITE OWL

WHITE SWINGS

RED CHEERS

RED NECKS

RED BIRDS

BLACKS RISE

BLACKS MARCH

WHITE LUST

WHITE ILLNESS

WHITE FETISH

BLACK PEACE

BLACK GRACE

MORE LOVE

MORE LOVE

EARTH LEARNS

EARTH GROWS

CIVIL REIGNS

LA NEGRITUDAMOS

BLACK BEANS

BLACK RICE

BLACK SOAP

BLACK CONES

BLACK ANGELS

BLACK SPIDERS

BLACK DUST

BLACK TUSKS

BLACK ELVIS

BLACK FLOORS

BLACK TILES

BLACK HAIR

BLACK LIGHTS

BLACK DANCERS

BLACK ZOMBIES

BLACK ANGST

BLACK HEELS

BLACK HOODIES

BLACK TIMBS

BLACK CHUCKS

BLACK BALLYS

BLACK DENIM

BLACK DRESS

BLACK BARS

BLACK CLUBS

BLACK DUDES

BLACK CHICKS

BLACK BANKERS

BLACK DENTISTS

BLACK DOCTORS

BLACK ACTORS

BLACK ADMEN

BLACK DANCESTRESS

BLACK SINGERS

BLACK CREATIVES

BLACK TEACHERS

BLACK WRITERS

BLACK COUNCILS

BLACK MAYORS

BLACK PARLIAMENT

BLACK CHAMBERS

BLACK PRESIDENTS

PRIME MINISTERS

BLACK DEACONS

BLACK CARDINALS

BLACK NUNS

BLACK LEADERS

BLACK LAUGHS

BLACKSTREET

BLACK LOVE

BLACK MICE

BLACKBIRDS

BLACK BEARS

BLACK SWANS

BLACK JESUS

BLACK CLOUDS

BLACK ICE

SKY HIGH, SKY HIGH

THE STERLING

THIS DRY NOTE DEPRECIATED ON THE OUTSIDE

WAY BEFORE THE CURRENCY RODE A DEBT

THAT DEEPENED THE DIVIDE BETWEEN ITS CUSTOMERS

THE ANALYSTS FEIGNED LOVE FOR THE SIGNATURE

THE MANAGEMENT SPECULATED ON THE BONDS

THE NOTES HAD A FUNNY VALUATION METRIC

THE NOTE DID NOT HIGHLY RATE CONSUMER PROFITS

CONSUMERS DIDN'T ASK HIM TO OVERSELL NEGATIVE INDEX RATINGS

THE NOTE USED PROFITS TO PREACH A STRONG BUY

HEDGING THAT WHAT WE KNEW WOULD NOT MATTER OR MIND

FUNDING THE LOGO LOCKED IN A FIXED RATE

THE DIRECTIONAL BIAS NEEDED NO FORECAST

UNTIL THE VENDOR RECORDED ILLEGAL INSIDER INFORMATION

SPEEDING UP THE TIME HORIZON IN BEVERLY HILLS

OLD STERLINGS ARE VOLATILE BELOW THE COVER SHEET

A NOTE WITH LOW RELATIVE STRENGTH

THE VISOR GLOWS; MATURED?

SPONSORSHIP

THE PRESENT PARTICIPATION OF THE PEOPLE

LACKS PERFECTION IN THE PRESENT TIME

THAT MAY PAUSE THE PERCEPTION OF THE FUTURE

MAKING IT PLAINLY IMPERFECT

LIKE A POSTSCRIPT MISSING TWO PUNCTUALS

SEEING AN EXCLAMATION POINT MISSING ITS VERTICAL LINE

SOUNDING OUT AN AMPERSAND IN THESE PLACES

EARNING A PENCE BEFORE THE POUND

PREDICATED AT THE ALTAR OF THE VERB

SUBJECTED TO PRISONS OF DELUSION

FOUND IN A PRE-MILLENNIAL DISCOURSE

WHEN PRESIDENT PINOCHET PAID DUES

PUSHING PERSECUTION OF HIS OWN

PLEASING THE COFFERS OF THE PENTAGON

ON A POSTAGE SEAL, PEOPLES' DREAMS LAY ON A PLATTER

IS IT PLATED IN PENTECOSTAL GOLD? CAN IT IMPRESS?

WHILE THE SEAL OF OPPRESSION CIRCLES

PUBLIC DIN CAN'T PURSUE THE ANSWER

LEST WE PAY ATTENTION. POW!

MAKE VALUE, MAKE TIME

START LOOKING AHEAD

START THINKING FORWARD

START PAYING IT FORWARD

STOP LOOKING OVER YOUR SHOULDER

START SPREADING THE NEWS

START PREACHING YOUR GOSPEL

START POLITICKING FOR THE REVOLUTION

STOP TELLING ME AND WOMEN TO SMILE

START IMAGINING THE FUTURE

START POOLING YOUR FINANCES

START STITCHING THE FABRIC OF YOUR LIFE

STOP LYING THAT IT ISN'T ABOUT RACE

START THE DAY WITH A GLASS OF WATER

START YOUR MORNING WITH GREENS AND GRAINS

START YOUR PLATE WITH TOAST, EGG, AND CHEESE

STOP THE BULLSHIT THAT EATING HEALTHY IS CORNBALL

TRYNTA TO LIVE PAST YOU, DUMB MOTHAFUCKA

START TURNING THE CORNER ONTO NEW STREETS

START BUILDING WITH SMALL BUSINESS OWNERS

START BUILDING WITH BIG BUSINESS OWNERS

STOP SUPPORTING ENTITIES THAT WANT TO KILL YOU

LITERALLY AND FIGURATIVELY

START BEING THE FIFTH ONE AT THE BARBER SHOP

START BEING THE FIRST ONE TO LEAVE THE HAIR SALON

START BEING THE BEST GIFTER TO FEEL YOUNG, BLACK, AND GIFTED

STOP ACTING A FOOL AT ALL TIMES

NOT MY FAULT THAT YOU SHOOK IN YOUR EMOTIONS

START LEARNING ABOUT THE VALUE OF HEMP

START UNDERSTANDING THE WAR ON DRUGS

START FOLLOWING BREE NEWSOME AND TEF POE ON TWITTER

STOP PLEADING PEACE WHEN NO JUSTICE EXISTS IN OUR SOCIETY

START PAYING ATTENTION TO AFRICA, ASIA AND THE MIDDLE EAST

START UNDERSTANDING HOW THEY INFLUENCED WESTERN CIVILIZATION

START REVIEWING THE WAR AGAINST ALL PUERTO RICANS

STOP SNITCHING ON YOURSELF

DAMN GOD

ULTRA MODERN IDIOMS

THIRST

WANT FOR LOVE OR LUST

SEE IT ALL

SIP IT SOME

DO IT ONCE IN THE MIND NOW

SHADE

ACTS OF DISS AND DEATH

THROW IT HARD

96

PUMPING SWEAT ON THE BACKSIDE

PETTY

GASEOUS

HELIUM

BLOWING UP

FUCK YOUR HURT

TAKE YOUR TALK TO THE BACK HAND

BANANAS

SLIP

SLIP & SLIDE

PEEL ON DOWN

SPLIT THE BIT

OPEN UP

SHUT EYE

WOW

FOH

FUCK OUTTA HERE, FOOL!

TRYNTA FUCK SHIT

OUTTA TIME

NO FUCKS GIVEN

COLD

ICY HOT

ASHY KNEES

SPASMED BACK

BROKEN TOES

FROM THAT PORCH TALK

S'LIT

OFF THE CHAIN

PLASMA STOPS

MERKING COPS

SPITTING UP AT BIG BEN

TITLED

WHY THE FUSS?

IN THE FACE?

PULL THAT OUT

FROM MY EYE

SOPHOMORE STAN

GET ON GONE

FORE YOU GET GOT

WHO'S THE BEST?

WHO'S THE WORST?

YOU SAID WHAT?

WHAT THE FUCK?

NIGGA WHAT?

NIGGA WHO?

CRACKA WHAT?

CRACKA WHO?

REALLY BISH?

OKAY, THUMB THUG

TRY IT THEN

CAN'T SEE ME

KNOW THIS SHIT

WHAT WILL BE

HOW IT DO

SALUDO

YA NO QUIERE

<u>ELLIPSES</u>.....

TIME IS NOTHING MORE THAN A POINT OF VIEW FILLED WITH REFERENCES THAT
YOU CAN USE OR LOSE......

NEED AN EXTENSION? VISIT EXTENDEDSYLLABLES.COM FOR PERFORMANCE HIGH-LIGHTS AND MUSIC DOWNLOADS!

CPSIA information can be obtained
at www.ICGtesting.com
Printed in the USA
LVHW091715170619
621482LV00004B/852/P